PERIOD OF ADJUSTMENT

By TENNESSEE WILLIAMS

PLAYS

Baby Doll (a screenplay)
Camino Real
Cat on a Hot Tin Roof
The Glass Menagerie
Orpheus Descending
The Rose Tattoo
A Streetcar Named Desire
Suddenly Last Summer
Summer and Smoke
Sweet Bird of Youth
27 Wagons Full of Cotton and Other Plays
You Touched Me (with Donald Windham)

POETRY

Five Young American Poets, 1944
In the Winter of Cities

PROSE

The Roman Spring of Mrs. Stone
One Arm and Other Stories
Hard Candy and Other Stories

PERIOD OF ADJUSTMENT

High Point over a Cavern

A SERIOUS COMEDY

by TENNESSEE WILLIAMS

A NEW DIRECTIONS BOOK

To the director and the cast

Period of Adjustment was presented at the Helen Hayes Theatre in New York on November 10, 1960, by Cheryl Crawford. It was directed by George Roy Hill; the stage settings and lighting were by Jo Mielziner and the costumes by Patricia Zipprodt; production stage manager, William Chambers. The cast, in order of appearance, was as follows:

RALPH BATES	JAMES DALY
ISABEL HAVERSTICK	BARBARA BAXLEY
GEORGE HAVERSTICK	ROBERT WEBBER
SUSIE	HELEN MARTIN
LADY CAROLER	ESTHER BENSON
MRS. McGILLICUDDY	NANCY R. POLLOCK
MR. McGILLICUDDY	LESTER MACK
THE POLICE OFFICER	CHARLES MC DANIEL
DOROTHY BATES	ROSEMARY MURPHY

PERIOD OF ADJUSTMENT

The Scene

The action of the play takes place in Ralph Bates' home in a suburb of a mid-southern city. The time is Christmas Eve.

ACT ONE

The set is the interior and entrance of a "cute" little Spanish-type suburban bungalow. Two rooms are visible onstage, the living room with its small dining alcove and the bedroom. There are doors to the kitchen and bath. A bit of the stucco exterior surrounds the entrance, downstage right or left. A Christmas wreath is on the door, while above the door is an ornamental porch light, or coach lantern, with amber glass or possibly glass in several colors. The fireplace in the fourth wall of the set is represented by a flickering red light. Of course the living room contains a TV set with its back to the audience, its face to a big sofa that opens into a bed. The dog is a cocker spaniel. There's a rather large Christmas tree, decorated, with a child's toys under it and a woman's fur coat in an open box, but no child and no woman. RALPH BATES, a boyish-looking man in his middle thirties, is approaching the TV set, facing upstage, with a can of beer and opener.

TV COMMERCIAL: Millions of Americans each day are discovering the difference between this new miracle product and the old horse-and-buggy type of cleanser which made washday a torture to Mom and left her too tired at sundown to light up the house with the sunshine of her smile.

RALPH: *No snow!*

[*He hoists himself onto a very high bar stool facing the TV.*]

TV COMMERCIAL: So don't let unnecessary fatigue cast a shadow over your household, especially not at this—

[*He leaps off the stool and crouches to change the channel. He gets snatches of several dramatic and musical offerings, settles for a chorus of "White Christmas," sighs, picks up a poker and stabs at the flickering ruddy light in the fourth wall. It comes up brighter. He crouches to fan the fire with*]

3

an antique bellows: the fire brightens. He sighs again, hoists himself back onto the brass-studded red-leather-topped stool, which has evidently been removed from the "cute" little bar, which is upstage. For theatrical purpose, this stool is about half a foot higher than any other sitting-surface on the stage. Whenever RALPH *assumes a seat on this stool he is like a judge mounting his judicial bench, except he's not pompous or bewigged about it. He is detached, considering, thinking, and over his face comes that characteristic look of a gentle gravity which is the heart of* RALPH. *Perhaps his pose should suggest Rodin's "Thinker."* RALPH *is one of those rare people that have the capacity of heart to truly* care, *and care deeply, about other people.*

{A car horn, urgent, is heard out front, offstage. RALPH *slides off the stool and rushes out the front door; he stands under the amber coach lantern. It's snowing, the snowflakes are projected on his figure, tiny, obliquely falling particles of shadow. There's a muffled shout from the car that's stopped below the terrace of the bungalow.}*

RALPH [*shouting back*]: Hey, there, drive her up under th' carport!

GEORGE [*Texas voice*]: Whacha say, boy?

RALPH: PUT 'ER UNDER THE CARPORT!

GEORGE: Wheels won't catch, too steep!

RALPH: Back her all the way out and then shoot 'er up in first!

ISABEL'S VOICE [*high-pitched with strain*]: Will you please let me out first, George!

[*There is the sound of a car door.* RALPH *ducks back in, grinning, and seizes a carton of rice.*]

RALPH: Yeah, come on in, little lady.

4

[ISABEL *appears before the house, small and white-faced with fatigue, eyes dark-circled, manner dazed and uncertain. She wears a cheap navy-blue cloth coat, carries a shiny new patent-leather purse, has on red wool mittens.* RALPH *pelts her with rice. She ducks the bombardment with a laugh that's more like a sob.*]

ISABEL: Oh, no, please! I never want to see rice again in my life, not uncooked anyhow. . . . That fire looks wonderful to me. I'm Isabel Crane, Mr. Bates.

[*She removes a red mitten and extends her hand.*]

RALPH: I thought you'd married that boy.

[*Both speak in deep Southern voices; hers is distinctly Texan.*]

ISABEL: I mean Mrs. George Haverstick.

[*She says her new name with a hint of grimness.*]

RALPH [*still in the door*]: Wait'll I put m'shoes on, I'll come out!

[*This shout is unheard.*]

ISABEL: You have a sweet little house.

RALPH [*with a touch of amiable grimness*]: Yeah, we sure do. Wheels cain't git any traction, 'stoo damn steep.

[*He shouts down.*]

LOCK IT UP, LEAVE IT OUT FRONT!—I guess he's gonna do that, yep, that's what he's doin', uh-huh, that's what he's doin. . . .

ISABEL: Does it snow often in Dixon?

RALPH: No, no, rarely, rarely.

5

[He gives her a glance. RALPH *has a sometimes discon-certing way of seeming either oblivious to a person he's with or regarding the person with a sudden intense concen-tration, as if he'd just noticed something startling or puz-zling about them. But this is a mannerism that the actor should use with restraint.]*

ISABEL: It was snowing all the way down here; it's my first acquaintance with snow except for one little flurry of snow in Saint Louis the day befo' Thanksgivin' day, this is my first real acquaintance with, with—with a real *snow*. . . . What *is* he doing down there?

RALPH: He's unloadin' th' car.

ISABEL: I just want my small zipper bag. Will you please call down to him that's all I want of my things?

RALPH *[shouting]*: Leave all that stuff till later. Ha ha. I didn't know you could get all that in a car.

ISABEL: Surely he isn't removing our wedding presents! Is he *insane*, Mr. Bates?

[She goes to the door.]

George! Just my small zipper bag, not everything in the car! Oh, Lord.

[She retreats into the room.]

He must think we're going to *live* here for the rest of our *lives!* He didn' even warn you all we were coming.

RALPH: He called me up from West Dixon.

ISABEL: Yes, just across the river.

RALPH: What is that car, a Caddy?

ISABEL: It's a fifty-two Cadillac with a mileage close to a hundred and twenty thousand. It ought to be retired with an old-age pension, Mr. Bates.

RALPH [*at the door*]: It looks like one of them funeral limousines.

ISABEL [*wryly*]: Mr. Bates, you have hit the nail on the head with the head of the hammer. That is just what it was. It's piled up a hundred and twenty thousand miles between Burkemeyer's Mortuary and various graveyards serving Greater Saint Louis. JAWGE, CAN YOU HEAR ME, JAWGE? Excuse me, Mr. Bates.

[*She slips past him onto the terrace again.*]

JAWGE, JUST MY SMALL ZIPPER BAG.

[*Indistinct shout from below. She turns back in.*]

I give up, Mr. Bates.

[*She ducks under his arm to enter the house again and stands behind Ralph in the doorway.*]

RALPH [*still chuckling at the door*]: What's he want with a funeral limousine? On a honeymoon trip?

ISABEL: I asked him that same question and got a very odd answer. He said there's no better credit card in the world than driving up at a bank door in a Cadillac limousine.

[*She tries to laugh.*]

Oh, I don't know, I—love Spanish-type architecture, Spanish mission-type houses, I—don't think you ought to stand in that door with just that light shirt on you, this is a—such a —*sweet* house. . . .

[*She seems close to tears. Something in her tone catches his attention and he comes in, closing the door.*]

7

RALPH: Ha, ha, well, how's it going? Is the marriage in orbit?

ISABEL [*tries to laugh at this, too*]: Oh! Will you please do me a favor? Don't encourage him, please don't invite him to spend the night here, Mr. Bates! I'm thinking of your wife, because last night—in Cape Girardeau, Missouri?—he thought it would be very nice to look up an old war buddy he had there, too. He sincerely thought so, and possibly the war buddy thought so, too, but NOT the wife! Oh, no, not *that* lady, no! They'd hardly got through their first beer cans with—remembrances of Korea, when that bright little woman began to direct us to a highway motel which she said was only a hop, skip and jump from their house but turned out to be almost across the state line into—Arkansas? Yaias, Arkansas. I think I can take this off, now!

[*She removes a red woolen muffler. He takes it from her and she murmurs "Thanks."*]

What is holding him up? Why is he—? Mr. Bates, I did tell him that this is one night of the year when you just don't intrude on another young married couple.

RALPH: Aw, come off that, little lady! Why, I been beggin' that boy ever since we got out of the service to come to Dixon. He had to git married to make it. Why, every time I'd git drunk, I'd call that boy on the phone to say "Git to hell down here, you old Texas jack rabbit!" And I'd just about given up hope he'd ever show!

ISABEL: Is he still fooling with luggage?

[*There is a noise outside.* RALPH *goes to the open door.*]

RALPH: *Hey!*

ISABEL: *What?*

RALPH: Ha ha ha! He put these bags at the door and run back down to the car.

ISABEL: *What* did he—?

RALPH: Gone back down for more luggage. I'll take these in.

ISABEL [*as the bags are brought in*]: Those are *my* pieces of luggage! All but the small zipper bag which is all that I wanted!

RALPH [*calling out the open door*]: Hey!

ISABEL: *What?*

RALPH: *Hey, boy!* He's gotten back in the car an' driven *off*, ha ha!

ISABEL [*rushing to the door*]: *Driven? Off?* Did you say? My heavens. You're right, he's *gone!* Mr. Bates, he's *deposited me on your hands and driven away.*

[*She is stunned.*]

Oh, *how funny!* Isn't this *funny!*

[*Laughs wildly, close to sobbing.*]

It's no *surprise* to me, though! All the way down here from Cape Girardeau, where we stopped for our wedding night, Mr. Bates, I had a feeling that the first chance he got to, he would abandon me somewhere!

RALPH: Aw, now, take it easy!

ISABEL: That's what he's done! Put me and my bags in your hands and run away.

RALPH: Aw, now, no! The old boy wouldn't do that, ha ha, for Chrissakes. He just remembered something he had to, had to—go and get at a—drugstore.

ISABEL: If that was the case wouldn't he mention it to me?

RALPH: Aw now, I known that boy a long time and he's always been sort of way out, but never way out that far!

ISABEL: Where is your wife? Where's Mrs. Bates, Mr. Bates?

RALPH: Oh, she's not here, right now.

ISABEL: I'm SUCH A FOOL!

[*She giggles a little hysterically.*]

Oh, I'm such a *fool!* . . . Why didn't I know better, can you answer me that? . . . I hope the news of our approach didn't drive your wife away on Christmas eve, Mr. Bates. . . .

RALPH: No, honey.

ISABEL: He brought up everything but the little blue zipper bag which is all I asked faw! . . . It had my, all my, it had my—*night* things in it. . . .

RALPH: Just let me get you a drink. I'm sorry I don't have any egg nog. But I can make a wonderful hot buttered rum. How about a little hot buttered rum?

ISABEL: Thank you, no, I don't drink. . . .

RALPH: It's never too late to begin to.

ISABEL: No, I don't want liquor.

RALPH: Coffee? Want some hot coffee?

ISABEL: Where is your wife, Mr. Bates?

RALPH: Oh, she's—not here now, I'll tell you about that later.

ISABEL: She will be outraged. This is one night of the year when you don't want outside disturbances—on your hands. . . .

10

RALPH: I think I know what to give you.

ISABEL: I did expect it but yet I didn't expect it!—I mean it occurred to me, the possibility of it, but I thought I was just being morbid.

RALPH: Aw, now, I know that boy. We been through two wars together, took basic training together and officer's training together. He wouldn't ditch you like that unless he's gone crazy.

ISABEL: George Haverstick is a very sick man, Mr. Bates. He was a patient in neurological at Barnes Hospital in Saint Louis, that's how I met him. I was a student nurse there.

[*She is talking quickly, shrilly. She has a prim, severe manner that disguises her prettiness.*]

RALPH: Yeah? What was wrong with him in the hospital, honey?

ISABEL: If we see him again, if he ever comes back to this house, you will *see* what's wrong. *He shakes!* Sometimes it's just barely noticeable, just a constant, slight tremor, you know, a sort of—vibration, like a—like an electric vibration in his muscles or nerves?

RALPH: Aw. That old tremor has come back on him, huh? He had that thing in Korea.

ISABEL: How bad did he have it in Korea, Mr. Bates?

RALPH: You know—like a heavy drinker—except he didn't drink heavy.

ISABEL: It's like he had Parkinson's disease but he doesn't have it.

[*She speaks like an outraged spinster, which is quite incongruous to her pretty, childlike appearance.*]

11

RALPH: What in hell is it then?

ISABEL: THAT is a MYSTERY! He shakes, that's all. He just shakes. Sometimes you'd think that he was shaking to pieces. . . . Was that a car out front?

[*She goes to the window.*]

No! I've caught a head cold, darn it.

[*Blows her nose.*]

When I met Mr. George Haverstick—Excuse me, you're watching TV!

RALPH [*turning off set*]: Naw, I'm not watchin' TV.

ISABEL: I'm so wound up, sitting in silence all day beside my—silent bridegroom, I can't seem to stop talking now, although I—hardly know you. Yes. I met him at Barnes Hospital, the biggest one in Saint Louis, where I was taking my training as a nurse, he had gone in Barnes instead of the Veterans Hospital because in the Veterans Hospital they couldn't discover any physical cause of this tremor and he thought they just said there wasn't any physical cause in order to avoid having to pay him a physical disability—compensation! I had him as a patient at Barnes Hospital, on the night shift. My, did he keep me running! The little buzzer was never out of his hand. Couldn't sleep under any kind of sedation less than enough to knock an elephant out!—Well, that's where I met George, I was very touched by him, honestly, very, very touched by the boy! I thought he sincerely loved me. . . . Yes, I *have* caught a head cold, or am I crying? I guess it's fatigue—exhaustion.

RALPH: You're just going through a period of adjustment.

ISABEL: Of course at Barnes he got the same diagnosis, or lack of diagnosis, that he'd gotten at the Vets Hospital in

Korea and Texas and elsewhere, no physical basis for the tremor, perfect physical health, suggested—psychiatry to him! He blew the roof off! You'd think they'd accused him of beating up his grandmother, at least, if not worse! I swear! Mr. Bates, I still have sympathy for him, but it wasn't fair of him not to let me know he'd quit his job at the airfield till after our marriage. He gave me that information after the wedding, right after the wedding he told me, right on the bridge, Eads Bridge between Saint Louis and East Saint Louis, he said, "Little Bit? Take a good look at Saint Louie because it may be your last one!" I'm quoting him exactly, those were his words. I don't know why I didn't say drive me right back. . . . Isn't it strange that I didn't say turn around on the other side of this bridge and drive me right back? I gave up student nursing at a great hospital to marry a man not honest enough to let me know he'd given up his job till an hour after the wedding!

RALPH: George is a high-strung boy. But they don't make them any better.

ISABEL: A man's opinion of a man! If they don't make them any better than George Haverstick they ought to stop production!

[RALPH *throws back his head, laughing heartily.*]

No, I mean it, if they don't make them better than a man that would abandon his bride in less than—how many hours? —on the doorstep of a war buddy and drive on without her or any apology to her, if that's the best they make them, I say *don't make them!*

[*There is a pause. She has crouched before the fire again, holding her hands out to the flickering glow.*]

Did George tell you on the phone that he's quit his job?

RALPH [*pouring brandy*]: What job did he quit, honey?

ISABEL: He was a ground mechanic at Lambert's airfield in Saint Louis. I had lost my job too, I hadn't quit, no, I was politely dismissed. My first day in surgery?—I *fainted!*—when the doctor made the incision and I saw the blood, I keeled over. . .

RALPH: That's understandable, honey.

ISABEL: Not in a nurse, not in a girl that had set her heart on nursing, that—how long has he been gone?

RALPH: Just a few minutes, honey. Xmas Eve traffic is heavy and George being George, he may have stopped at a bar on his way back here. . . . You'd been going steady how long?

ISABEL: Ever since his discharge from Barnes Hopsital. Isn't this suburb called High Point?

RALPH: Yes. High Point over a cavern.

ISABEL: His place was in High Point, too. Another suburb called High Point, spelled Hi dash Point—hyphenated.

RALPH: I guess all fair-sized American cities have got a suburb called High Point, hyphenated or not, but this is the only one I know of that's built on a cavern.

ISABEL [*without really listening to him*]: Cavern?

[*She laughs faintly as if it were a weak joke.*]

Well, I said, George, on the bridge, we're not driving down to Florida in that case. We're going to find you a job; we're going from city to city until you find a new job and I don't care if we cross the Rio Grande, we're not going to stop until you find one! Did I or didn't I make the right decision? In your opinion, Mr. Bates.

RALPH: Well. How did he react to it?

14

ISABEL: Stopped talking and started shaking! So violently I was scared he would drive that funeral car off the road! Ever since then it's been hell! And I am—

[*She springs up from the fireplace chair.*]

—not exactly the spirit of Christmas, am I?

[*She goes to the window to look out; sees nothing but windy snow. There is a low rumble. A picture falls off the wall.*]

What was that?

RALPH: Oh, nothing. The ground just settled a little We get that all the time here because this suburb, High Point, is built over a great big underground cavern and is sinking into it gradually, an inch or two inches a year. It would cost three thousand dollars to stabilize the foundation of this house even temporarily! But it's not publicly known and we homeowners and the promoters of the project have got together to keep it a secret till we have sold out, in alphabetical order, at a loss but not a complete sacrifice. Collusion, connivance. Disgusting but necessary.

[*She doesn't hear this, murmurs "What?" as she crosses back to the window at the sound of a car going by.*]

ISABEL: It's funny, I had a hunch he was going to leave me somewhere.

[*She laughs sadly, forlornly, and lets the white window curtains fall together.*]

RALPH: Why don't you take off your coat and sit back down by the fire? That coat keeps the heat off you, honey. That boy's comin' back.

ISABEL: Thank you.

[*She removes her coat.*]

RALPH [*observing with solemn appreciation the perfect neatness of her small body*]: I'm *sure* that boy's coming back. I am now *positive* of it! That's a cute little suit you're wearing. Were you married in that?

ISABEL: Yes, I was married in this traveling suit. Appropriately.

RALPH: You couldn't have looked any prettier in white satin.

[RALPH *is at the bar preparing a snifter of brandy for her. Now he puts a match to it and as it flares up blue, she cries out a little.*]

ISABEL: What is, what are you—?

RALPH: Something to warm up your insides, little lady.

ISABEL: Well, isn't that sweet of you? Will it burn if I touch it?

RALPH: Naw, naw, naw, take it, take it.

ISABEL: Beautiful. Let me hold it to warm my hands first, before I—

[*He puts the snifter glass of blue-flaming brandy in her hands and they return to the fireplace.*]

I'm not a drinker, I don't think doctors or nurses have any right to be, but I guess *now*—I'm *out* of the nursing profession! *So* . . . What a sweet little bar. What a sweet little house. And such a sweet Christmas tree.

RALPH: Yeah. Everything's sweet here. I married a homely girl, honey, but I tried to love her.

[ISABEL *doesn't really hear this remark.*]

ISABEL: I hope your wife didn't take your little boy out because we were coming.

16

RALPH: I sure did make an effort to love that woman. I almost stopped realizing that she was homely.

ISABEL: So he didn't actually tell you he was going to a drugstore, Mr. Bates?

RALPH [*uncomfortably*]: He didn't say so. I just figured he was.

ISABEL: I—well, he's abandoned me here.

RALPH: How long've you known George?

ISABEL: I'm afraid I married a stranger.

RALPH: Everybody does that.

ISABEL: Where did you say your wife was?

RALPH: My wife has quit me.

ISABEL: No! You're joking, aren't you?

RALPH: She walked out on me this evening when I let her know I'd quit my job.

ISABEL [*beginning to listen to him*]: Surely it's just temporary, Mr. Bates.

RALPH: Nope. Don't think so. I quit my job and so my wife quit me.

ISABEL: I don't think a woman leaves a man as nice as you, Mr. Bates, for such a reason as that.

RALPH: Marriage is an economic arrangement in many ways, let's face it, honey. Also, the situation between us was complicated by the fact that I worked for her father. But that's another story. That's a long other story and you got your mind on George.

ISABEL: I think my pride has been hurt.

17

RALPH: I told you he's coming back and I'm just as sure of it as I'm sure Dorothea isn't. Or if she does, that she'll find me waiting for her. Ohhhhh, nooooo! I'm cutting out of this High Point over a Cavern on the first military transport I can catch out of Dixon.

ISABEL [*vaguely*]: You don't mean that, Mr. Bates, you're talking through your hat, out of hurt feelings, hurt pride.

[*She opens the front door and stands looking out as forlornly as a lost child. She really does have a remarkably cute little figure and* RALPH *takes slow, continual and rather wistful stock of it with his eyes.*]

RALPH: I got what I had comin' to me, that I admit, for marryin' a girl that didn't attract me.

[*He comes up behind her at the door.*]

ISABEL: Did you say didn't attract you?

RALPH: Naw, she didn't attract me in the beginning. She's one year older'n me and I'm no chicken. But I guess I'm not the only man that would marry the only daughter of an old millionaire with diabetes and gallstones and one kidney. Am I?

ISABEL: It's nice out here.

RALPH: But I'm telling you I'm convinced there is no greater assurance of longevity in this world than one kidney, gallstones an' diabetes! That old man has been cheating the undertaker for yea many years. Seems to thrive on one kidney and . . .

[*He tosses the beer can down the terrace.*]

Oh, they live on anything—nothing!

ISABEL: Do you always throw beer cans on your front lawn, Mr. Bates?

18

RALPH: Never before in my life. I sure enjoyed it. George is gonna be shocked when he sees me. I sacrificed my youth to—

ISABEL: What?

RALPH: Yep, it's nice out here. I mean, nicer than in there.

ISABEL: You sacrificed your youth?

RALPH: Oh, that. Yeah! I'll tell you more about that unless it bores you.

ISABEL: No.

RALPH: She had fallen into the hands of a psychiatrist when I married this girl. This psychiatrist was charging her father fifty dollars a session to treat her for a condition that he diagnosed as "psychological frigidity." She would shiver violently every time she came within touching distance of a possible boy friend. Well—I think the psychiatrist misunderstood her shivers.

ISABEL: She might have shivered because of—

RALPH: That's what I *mean!* Why, the night I met her, I heard a noise like castanets at a distance. I thought some Spanish dancers were about to come on! Ha ha! Then I noticed her teeth—she had buck teeth at that time which were later extracted!—were chattering together and her whole body was uncontrollably shaking!

ISABEL: We both married into the shakes! But Mr. Bates, I don't think it's very nice of you to ridicule the appearance of your wife.

RALPH: Oh, I'm not!

ISABEL: You WERE!

RALPH: At my suggestion she had the buck teeth extracted. It was like kissing a rock pile before the extractions! I swear!

19

ISABEL: Now, Mr. Bates.

RALPH: This snow almost feels warm as white ashes out of a—chimney.

ISABEL: Excuse me. I'll get my—sweater.

[*She goes in. He remains on the little paved terrace. When she comes out again in her cardigan, he goes on talking as if there'd been no interruption.*]

RALPH: Yep, her old man was payin' this head-shrinker fifty dollars per session for this condition he diagnosed as "psychological frigidity." I cured her of that completely almost overnight. But at thirty-seven, my age, you ain't middle-aged but you're in the shadow of it and it's a spooky shadow. I mean, when you look at *late* middle-aged couples like the McGillicuddys, my absent wife's parents . . .

ISABEL: Mr. Bates, don't you think I should go downtown and take a hotel room? Even if George comes back, he ought not to find me here like a checked package waiting for him to return with the claim check. Because if you give up your pride, what are you left with, really?

[*She turns and goes back inside. He follows her in. Immediately after they enter, a* NEGRO GIRL *appears on the terrace.*]

Don't you agree, Mr. Bates?

[*The* GIRL *rings the doorbell.*]

RALPH: *Here he is now. You see?*

[ISABEL, *who had sunk onto a hassock before the fireplace, now rises tensely as* RALPH *calls out:*]

COME ON IN, LOVER BOY! THAT DOOR AIN'T LOCKED!

[RALPH *opens the door.*]

20

Oh . . . What can I do fo' you, Susie?

[SUSIE *comes into the room with a sheepish grin.*]

SUSIE: 'Scuse me for comin' to the front door, Mr. Bates, but that snow's wet and I got a hole in muh shoe!

RALPH: You alone?

SUSIE: Yes, suh.

RALPH: They sent you for somethin'?

SUSIE: Yes, suh, they sent me faw th' chile's Santie Claus.

RALPH: Aw, they did, huh? Well, you go right back an' tell the McGillicuddys that "the chile's Santie Claus" is stayin' right here till the chile comes over for it, because I bought it, not them, and I am at least *half* responsible for the "chile's" existence, *also.* Tell them the chile did not come into the world without a father and it's about time for the chile to acknowledge that fact and for them to acknowledge that fact and— How did you git here, Susie?

SUSIE: Charlie brought me.

RALPH: Who's Charlie?

SUSIE: Charlie's they new *showfer,* Mr. Bates.

RALPH: Aw. Well, tell my wife and her folks, the McGillicuddys, that I won't be here tomorrow but "the chile's Santie Claus" will be here under the tree and say that I said Merry Christmas. Can you remember all that?

SUSIE: Yes, suh.

[*She turns and shouts through the door:*] Charlie! Don't come up, I'm comin' right down, Charlie!

[*The sound of a Cadillac motor starting is heard below the terrace as* SUSIE *leaves.* RALPH *looks out of the open door till the car is gone, then slams it shut.*]

RALPH: Dig that, will yuh! Sent a colored girl over to collect the kid's Christmas! This is typical of the Stuart McGillicuddys. I'd like to have seen Mr. Stuart McGillicuddy, the look on his face, when that Western Union messenger give him my message of resignation this afternoon and he was at last exposed to my true opinions of him!

ISABEL: You should have let her take the child's Christmas to it.

RALPH: They'll be over. Don't worry. And—I will be waiting for them with both barrels, man—will I blast 'em! Think of the psychiatrist fees that I saved her fat-head father! I even made her think that she was attractive, and over a five-year period got one pay raise when she give birth to my son which she has turned to a sissy.

[ISABEL *hasn't listened to his speech.*]

ISABEL: I thought that was George at the door. . . .

RALPH: That's life for you.

ISABEL: What?

RALPH: I said isn't that life for you!

ISABEL: *What* is life for us *all*?

[*She sighs.*]

My philosophy professor at the Baptist college I went to, he said one day, "We are all of us born, live and die in the shadow of a giant question mark that refers to three questions: Where do we *come* from? *Why? And where, oh where, are we going!*"

RALPH: When did you say you got married?

ISABEL: Yesterday. Yesterday morning.

RALPH: That lately? Well, he'll be back before you can say—Joe Blow.

[*He appreciates her neat figure again.*]

ISABEL: What?

RALPH: Nothing.

ISABEL: Well!

RALPH: D'you like Christmas music?

ISABEL: Everything but "White Christmas."

[*As she extends her palms to the imaginary fireplace,* RALPH *is standing a little behind her, still looking her up and down with solemn appreciation.*]

RALPH: Aw, y' don't like "White Christmas"?

ISABEL: The radio in that car is practically the only thing in it that *works!* We had it on all the time.

[*She gives a little tired laugh.*]

Conversation was impossible, even if there had been a desire to talk! It kept playing "White Christmas" because it was snowing I guess all the way down here, yesterday and—today. . . .

RALPH: A radio in a funeral limousine?

ISABEL: I guess they just played it on the way back from the graveyard. Anyway, once I reached over and turned the volume down. He didn't say anything, he just reached over and turned the volume back up. Isn't it funny how a little thing like that can be so insulting to you? Then I started crying and still haven't stopped! I pretended to be looking out the car window till it got dark.

RALPH: You're just going through a little period of adjustment to each other.

23

ISABEL: What do you do with a bride left on your doorstep, Mr. Bates?

RALPH: Well, I, *ha ha*!—never *had* that experience!

ISABEL: Before? Well, now you're faced with it, I hope you know how to handle it. You know why I know he's left me? He only took in my bags, he left his own in the car, he brought in all of mine except my little blue zipper overnight bag, *that* he kept for some reason. Perhaps he intends to pick up another female companion who could use its contents.

RALPH: Little lady, you're in a bad state of nerves.

ISABEL: Have you ever been so tired that you don't know what you're doing or saying?

RALPH: Yes. Often.

ISABEL: That's my condition, so make allowances for it. Yes, indeed, that *sure* is a mighty *far* drugstore. . . .

[*She wanders back to the window, and parts the curtain to peer out.*]

RALPH: He seems gone twice as long because you're thinking about it.

ISABEL: I don't know why I should care except for my overnight bag with my toilet articles in it.

RALPH [*obliquely investigating*]: Where did you spend last night?

ISABEL [*vaguely*]: Where did we spend last night?

RALPH: Yeah. Where did you stop for the night?

ISABEL [*rubbing her forehead and sighing with perplexity*]: In a, in a—oh, a tourist camp called the—Old Man River Motel? Yes, the Old Man River Motel.

24

RALPH: That's a mistake. The first night ought to be spent in a real fine place regardless of what it cost you. It's so important to get off on the right foot.

[*He has freshened his drink and come around to the front of the bar. She has gone back to the window at the sound of a car.*]

If you get off on the wrong foot, it can take a long time to correct it.

[*She nods in slow confirmation of this opinion.*]

Um-hmmm. Walls are built up between people a hell of a damn sight faster than—broken down. . . . Y'want me to give you my word that he's coming back? I will, I'll give you my word. Hey.

[*He snaps his fingers.*]

Had he brought me a Christmas present? If not, *that's* what he's doing. *That* explains where he went to.

[*There is a pause. She sits sadly by the fireplace.*]

What went wrong last night?

ISABEL: Let's not talk about that.

RALPH: I don't mean to pry into such a private, intimate thing, but—

ISABEL: No, let's don't! I'll just put it this way and perhaps you will understand me. In spite of my being a student nurse, till discharged—my experience has been limited, Mr. Bates. Perhaps it's because I grew up in a small town, an only child, too protected. I wasn't allowed to date till my last year at High and then my father insisted on meeting the boys I went out with and laid down pretty strict rules, such as when to bring me home from parties and so forth. If he smelled liquor

25

on the breath of a boy? At the door? That boy would not enter the door! And that little rule ruled out a goodly number.

RALPH: I bet it did. They should've ate peanuts befo' they called for you, honey.

[*He chuckles, reflectively poking at the fire.*]

That's what we done at the Sisters of Mercy Orphans' Home in Mobile.

ISABEL [*touched*]: Oh. Were you an *orphan*, Mr. Bates?

RALPH: Yes, I had that advantage.

[*He slides off the high stool again to poke at the fire. She picks up the antique bellows and fans the flames, crouching beside him.*]

ISABEL: So you were an orphan! People that grow up orphans, don't they value love more?

RALPH: Well, let's put it this way. They get it less easy. To get it, they have to give it: so, yeah, they do value it more.

[*He slides back onto the bar stool. She crouches at the fireplace to fan the fire with the bellows; the flickering light brightens their shy, tender faces.*]

ISABEL: But it's also an advantage to have a parent like my daddy.

[*She's again close to tears.*]

Very strict but devoted. Opposed me going into the nursing profession but I had my heart set on it, I thought I had a vocation, I saw myself as a Florence Nightingale nurse. A lamp in her hand? Establishin' clinics in the—upper Amazon country. . . .

[*She laughs a little ruefully.*]

Yais, I had heroic daydreams about myself as a dedicated young nurse working side by side with a—

[*She pauses shyly.*]

RALPH: With a dedicated young doctor?

ISABEL: No, the doctor would be older, well, not too old, but—older. I saw myself passing among the pallets, you know, the straw mats, administering to the plague victims in the jungle, exposing myself to contagion. . . .

[*She exhibits a bit of humor here.*]

RALPH: *Catchin'* it?

ISABEL: Yais, contractin' it eventually *m'self.* . . .

RALPH: What were the symptoms of it?

ISABEL: A slight blemish appearing on the—hands?

[*She gives him a darting smile.*]

RALPH [*joining in the fantasy with her*]: Which you'd wear gloves to conceal?

ISABEL: Yais, rubber gloves all the time.

RALPH: A crusty-lookin' blemish or more like a fungus?

[*They laugh together.*]

ISABEL: I don't think I—yais, I did, I imagined it being like *scaa-ales*! Like silver fish scales appearing on my hainds and then progressing gradually to the wrists and *fo'*-arms. . . .

RALPH: And the young doctor discovering you were concealing this condition?

ISABEL: The *youngish middle-aged* doctor, Mr. Bates! Yais, discovering I had contracted the plague myself and then a big scene in which she says, Oh, no, you mustn't touch me but he

27

seizes her passionately in his arms, of course, and—exposes himself to contagion.

[RALPH *chuckles heartily getting off stool to poke at the fire again. She joins him on the floor to fan the flames with the bellows.*]

ISABEL: And love is stronger than death. You get the picture?

RALPH: Yep, I've seen the picture.

ISABEL: We've had a good laugh together. You're a magician, Ralph, to make me laugh tonight in my present situation. George and I never laugh, we never laugh together. Oh, he makes JOKES, YAIS! But we never have a really genuine laugh together and that's a bad sign, I think, because I don't think a married couple can go through life without laughs together any more than they can without tears.

RALPH: Nope.

[*He removes his shoes.*]

Take your slippers off, honey.

ISABEL: I have the funniest sensation in the back of my head, like—

RALPH: Like a tight rope was coming unknotted?

ISABEL: Exactly! Like a tight rope was being unknotted!

[*He removes her slippers and puts them on the hearth, crosses into the bedroom and comes out with a pair of fluffy pink bedroom slippers. He crouches beside her and feels the sole of her stocking.*]

RALPH: Yep, damp. Take those damp stockings off.

ISABEL: [*unconsciously following the suggestion*]: Does George have a sense of humor? In your opinion? Has he got

28

the ability to laugh at himself and at life and at—human situations? Outside of off-color jokes? In your opinon, Mr. Bates?

RALPH [*taking the damp stockings from her and hanging them over the footlights*]: Yes. We had some good laughs together, me an'—"Gawge," ha ha. . . .

ISABEL: We never had any together.

RALPH: That's the solemnity of romantic love, little lady, I mean like Romeo and Juliet was not exactly a joke book, ha ha ha.

ISABEL: "The solemnity of romantic love"!—I wouldn't expect an old war buddy of George's to use an expression like that.

RALPH: Lemme put these on your feet, little lady.

[*She sighs and extends her feet and he slips the soft fleecy pink slippers on them.*]

But you know something? I'm gonna tell you something which isn't out of the joke books either. You got a wonderful boy in your hands, on your hands, they don't make them any better than him and I mean it.

[*He does.*]

ISABEL: I appreciate your loyalty to an old war buddy.

RALPH: Naw, naw, it's not just that.

ISABEL: But if they don't make them any better than George Haverstick, they ought to stop making them, they ought to *cease producing!*

[*She utters a sort of wild, sad laugh which stops as abruptly as it started. Suddenly she observes the bedroom slippers on her feet.*]

29

What's these, where did they come from?

RALPH: Honey, I just put them on you. Didn't you know?

ISABEL: No!—How strange!—I didn't, I wasn't at all aware of it. . . .

[*They are both a little embarrassed.*]

Where is your wife, Mr. Bates?

RALPH: Honey, I told you she quit me and went home to her folks.

ISABEL: Oh, excuse me, I remember. You told me. . . .

[*Suddenly the blazing logs make a sharp cracking noise; a spark apparently has spit out of the grate onto* ISABEL'S *skirt. She gasps and springs up, retreating from the fireplace, and* RALPH *jumps off the bar stool to brush at her skirt. Under the material of the Angora wool skirt is the equal and warmer softness of her young body.* RALPH *is abruptly embarrassed, coughs, turns back to the fireplace and picks up copper tongs to shift the position of crackling logs.*

[*This is a moment between them that must be done just right to avoid misinterpretation.* RALPH *would never make a play for the bride of a buddy. What should come out of the moment is not a suggestion that he will or might but that Dotty's body never felt that way. He remembers bodies that did. What comes out of Isabel's reaction is a warm understanding of his warm understanding; just that, nothing more, at all.*]

ISABEL: Thank you. This Angora wool is, is—highly inflammable stuff, at least I would—think it—might be. . . .

RALPH: Yeah, and I don't want "Gawge" to come back here and find, a toasted marshmallow bride . . . by my fireplace.

[*They sit down rather self-consciously,* RALPH *on the high stool,* ISABEL *on the low hassock.*]

ISABEL: Yais . . .

RALPH: Huh?

ISABEL: Daddy opposed me going into nursing so much that he didn't speak to me, wouldn't even look at me for a whole week before I took off for Saint Louie.

RALPH: Aw? Tch!

ISABEL: However, at the last moment, just before the train pulled out of the depot, he came stalking up the platform to the coach window with a gift package and an envelope. The package contained flannel nighties and the envelope had in it a list of moral instructions in the form of prayers such as: "O Heavenly Father, give thy weak daughter strength to—

[*She giggles.*]

—resist the—

[*She covers her mouth with a hand to suppress a spasm of laughter.*]

Oh, my Lord. Well, you would have to know Daddy to appreciate the—

RALPH: Honey, I reckon I know your daddy. That's what I meant about the orphan's advantage, honey.

[*They laugh together.*]

ISABEL: We sure do have some good laughs together, Mr. Bates. Now where did I get *these?*

[*She means the bedroom slippers.*]

These aren't mine, where did, how did—? *Oh—yes, you—*

[*They resume their grave contemplation of the fire.*]

"Heavenly Father, give thy weak daughter the strength of will to resist the lusts of men. Amen."

[RALPH *chuckles sadly.*]

And I was never tempted to, *not* to, resist them, till—George. . . .

RALPH: Did George arouse a—?

ISABEL: I don't suppose another man could see George the way I see him: SAW him. So *handsome?* And so *afflicted?* So afflicted and—*handsome?* With that mysterious *tremor?* With those SHAKES?

RALPH: How did "Jawge" come on?

ISABEL: Huh? Oh. No. I don't mean he came on like a—

RALPH: Bull? Exactly?

ISABEL: No, no, no, no. It was very strange, very—strange. . . .

RALPH: What?

ISABEL: He always wanted us to go out on double dates or with a whole bunch of—others. And when we were alone? Together? There was a—funny, oh, a very *odd*—sort of—*timidity!*—between us. . . . And that, of course is what touched me; oh, that—*touched* me. . . .

[*There is a pause in the talk.* RALPH *descends from his high perch and passes behind her low hassock with a smile behind her back which is a recognition of the truth of her romantic commitment to George. This is also in the slight, tender pat that he gives to the honey-colored crown of her head.*]

An so although I had many strong opportunities to give in to my "weakness" on, on—weekend dates with young interns and doctors at Barnes?—I was never tempted to do so. But with George—

RALPH: You did? Give in?

ISABEL: Mr. Bates, George Haverstick married a virgin, and I can't say for sure that it was my strength of will and not *his* that—deserves the credit. . . .

[RALPH *returns to fireplace with beer.*]

RALPH: Yeah, well. Now I'm going to tell you something about that boy that might surprise you after your experience last night at the Old Man River Motel.

[*He opens a beer can.*]

He always bluffs about his ferocious treatment of women, believe me! To hear him talk you'd think he spared them no pity! However, I happen to know he didn't come on as strong with those dolls in Tokyo and Hong Kong and Korea as he liked to pretend to. Because I heard from those dolls. . . . He'd just sit up there on a pillow and drink that rice wine with them and teach them *English*! Then come downstairs from there, hitching his belt and shouting, "*Oh, man! Oh, brother!*"—like he' laid 'em to waste.

ISABEL: That was not his behavior in the Old Man River Motel. Last night.

RALPH: What went wrong in the Old Man River Motel?

ISABEL: Too many men think that girls in the nursing profession must be—*shock*proof. I'm not, I wasn't—last night. . . .

RALPH: Oh. Was he drunk?

ISABEL: He'd been drinking all day in that heaterless retired funeral hack in a snowstorm to keep himself warm. Since I don't drink, I just had to endure it. Then. We stopped at the Old Man River Motel, as dreary a place as you could find on this earth! The electric heater in our cabin lit up but gave off no heat! Oh, *George* was comfortable there! Threw off his clothes and sat down in front of the heater as if I were not even present.

RALPH: Aw.

ISABEL: Continuing drinking!

RALPH: Aw.

ISABEL: Then began the courtship, and, oh, what a courtship it was, such tenderness, romance! I finally screamed. I locked myself in the bathroom and didn't come out till he had gotten to bed and then I—slept in a chair. . . .

RALPH: You wouldn't—

ISABEL: Mr. Bates, I just couldn't! The atmosphere just wasn't right. And he—

[*She covers her face.*]

—I can't tell you more about it just now except that it was a nightmare, him in the bed, pretending to be asleep, and me in the chair pretending to be asleep too and both of us knowing the other one *wasn't* asleep and, and, and—I can't tell you more about it right now, I just can't tell more than I've told you about it, I—

[*Her sobs become violent and there is a pause.*]

RALPH: Hey! Let me kiss the bride! Huh? Can I kiss the bride?

ISABEL: You're very kind, Mr. Bates. I'm sure you were more understanding with your wife when you were going through this—

RALPH: —period of adjustment? Yeah. That's all it is, it's just a little—period of adjustment.

[*He bestows a kiss on her tear-stained cheek and a pat on her head. She squeezes his hand and sinks down again before the fireplace.*]

ISABEL: It isn't as if I'd given him to believe that I was *experienced*! I made it clear that I *wasn't*. He knows my background and we'd talked at great *length* about my— inhibitions which I know are—*inhibitions,* but—which an understanding husband wouldn't expect his bride to overcome at *once,* in a tourist cabin, after a *long—silent—ride*!— in a *funeral hack* in a *snowstorm* with the *heater not working* in a *shocked*! *condition*!—having just been told that—we were *both* unemployed, and—

RALPH: Little Bit, Little Bit—you had a sleepless night in that motel—why don't you put in a little sack time now. You need it, honey. Take Dotty's bed in there and think about nothing till morning.

ISABEL: You mean you know, now, that George is not coming back?

RALPH: No. I mean that Dotty's not coming back.

ISABEL: I don't think you ever thought that he would come back for me any more than I did.

RALPH: Take Dotty's bed, get some sleep on that foam-rubber mattress while I sit here and watch the Late Late Show on TV.

ISABEL: But, Mister Bates, if your wife does come back here I wouldn't want her to find a stranger in your bedroom.

35

RALPH: Honey, finding a stranger in a bedroom is far from being the biggest surprise of a lifetime. So you go on in there and lock the door.

ISABEL: Thank you, Mister Bates.

[*She enters bedroom.*]

I'm only locking the door because of the slight possibility that Mister George Haverstick the fourth might come back drunk and try to repeat the comedy and tragedy of last night. I hope you realize that.

RALPH: Oh, sure. Good night, sleep tight, honey.

[*She locks the bedroom door as* RALPH *returns to the fireplace.*]

RALPH [*to himself and the audience*]: What a bitch of a Christmas.

CURTAIN

ACT TWO

No time lapse.

ISABEL *jumps up as a car is heard stopping out front. She looks wildly at* RALPH, *who gives her a nod and a smile as he crosses to the front door. Snow blows into the living room as he goes out and shouts:*

RALPH: HEY!

[ISABEL *catches her breath, waiting.*]
Ha ha!

[ISABEL *expels her breath and sits down.* RALPH, *shouting through snow:*]

Your wife thought she was deserted!

GEORGE [*from a distance*]: Hey!

[ISABEL *springs up and rushes to a mirror to wipe away tears.*

[*A car door is heard slamming in front of the house.* ISABEL *sits down. She immediately rises, rubbing her hands together, and then sits down again. Then she springs up and starts toward the bedroom. Stops short as*

[GEORGE *enters.*]

I'm the son of a camel, ha ha! My mother was a camel with two humps, a double hump—dromedary! Ha ha ha!

[GEORGE *and* RALPH *catch each other in a big, rocking hug.* ISABEL *stares, ignored, as the male greetings continue.*]

RALPH: *You ole son of a tail gun!*

GEORGE: *How'sa young squirrel? Ha ha!*

RALPH: *How'sa Texas jack rabbit?*

[*There is a sudden, incongruous stillness. They stare, all three of them,* ISABEL *at* GEORGE, GEORGE *and* RALPH *at each other.* GEORGE *is suddenly embarrassed and says:*]

GEORGE: Well, I see yuh still got yuh dawg.

RALPH: Yeah, m' wife's folks are cat lovers.

GEORGE: You'll get your wife back tomorrow.

RALPH: Hell, I don't want her back.

GEORGE: Y'don't want 'er back?

RALPH: That's right.

GEORGE: Hell, in that case, you won't be able to beat 'er off with a stick, ha ha!

[*His laugh expires as he catches* ISABEL'*s outraged look.*]

Won't be able to beat her away from the door with a stick t'morrow. . . .

[*They stare at each other brightly, with little chuckles, a constant series of little chuckles.* ISABEL *feels ignored.*]

ISABEL: I doubt that Mr. Bates means it.

GEORGE: Didn't you all have a kid of some kind? I don't remember if it was a boy or a girl.

ISABEL: The toys under the tree might give you a clue as to that.

RALPH: Yeah, it's a boy, I guess. Drink?

GEORGE: You bet.

[GEORGE *goes to the bar and starts mixing drinks.*]

ISABEL: How old is your little boy?

RALPH: Three years old and she's awready made him a sissy.

GEORGE: They'll do it ev'ry time, man.

[*He keeps chuckling, as does* RALPH.]

RALPH: I didn't want this kind of a dawg, either. I wanted a Doberman pinscher, a dawg with some guts, not a whiner! But she wanted a poodle and this flop-eared sad sack of a spaniel was a compromise which turned out to be worse'n a poodle, ha, ha. . . .

GEORGE: I'll bet yuh dollars to doughnuts your wife and kid'll be back here tomorrow.

RALPH [*in his slow drawl*]: They won't find me here if they do. I'm all packed to go. I would of been gone when you called but I'm waitin' t' git a call from a boy about t' git married. I want him to come over here an' make a cash offer on all this household stuff since I spent too much on Christmas and won't be around to collect my unemployment.

GEORGE: Come along with us. We got a big car out there an' we're as free as a breeze. Ain't that right, Little Bit?

ISABEL: Don't ask me what's right. I don't know! I *do* know, though, that couples with children don't separate at Christmas, and, George, let your friend work out his problems himself. You don't know the situation and don't have any right to interfere in it. And now will you please go get my little blue zipper bag for me? *Please?*

RALPH [*to* GEORGE, *as if she hadn't spoken*]: Naw, I'm just going out to the army airfield a couple miles down the highway and catch the first plane going west.

GEORGE: We'll talk about that.

ISABEL: *George!*

GEORGE: Aw, HERE! I forgot to give you your present! After drivin' almost back into Dixon to find a liquor store open.

[*He extends a gift-wrapped magnum of champagne.*]

RALPH: Lover Jesus, champagne?

GEORGE: Imported and already cold.

RALPH [*glancing briefly at* ISABEL]: Didn't I tell you that he was buyin' me something? She thought you'd deserted her, boy.

ISABEL: *All right, I'll get it myself! I'll go out and get it out of the car myself!*

[*She rushes out into snow, leaving the door open.*

[GEORGE *closes the door without apparently noticing her exit.*]

GEORGE: Boy, you an' me have got a lot to talk over.

RALPH: We sure got lots of territory to cover.

GEORGE: So your goddam marriage has cracked up on yuh, has it?

RALPH: How's yours goin'? So far?

GEORGE: We'll talk about it *later*. Discuss it *thoroughly! Later!*

RALPH: Y'got married yestiddy mawnin'?

GEORGE: Yeah.

RALPH: How was last night?

GEORGE: We'll talk about *that* later, too.

[ISABEL *rushes into the room in outrage, panting.*]

ISABEL: *I* can't break the lock on that *car*!

GEORGE: Little Bit, I didn't know that you wuh bawn in a barn.

[*He means she left the door open again.*]

ISABEL: I didn't know a lot about you, either!

[GEORGE *closes door.*]

Mr. Bates! Mr. Bates!

[*He turns toward her with a vague smile.*]

The gentleman I married refuses to get my zipper bag out of the car or unlock the car so I can get it myself.

[*The phone rings.* RALPH *picks it up.*]

RALPH [*in a slow, hoarse drawl, at the phone*]: Aw, hi, Smokey. I'm glad you got my message. Look. I quit Regal Dairy Products and I'm flyin' out of here late tonight or early tomorrow morning and I thought maybe you might like to look over some of my stuff here, the household equipment, and make me a cash offer for it. I'll take less in cash than a check since I'm not gonna stop at the Coast, I'm flying straight through to Hong Kong so it would be difficult for me to cash yuh check an' of course I expect to make a sacrifice on the stuff here. Hey! Would you like a beaver-skin coat, sheared beaver-skin coat for Gertrude? Aw. I'd let you have it for a, for a—third off! Aw. Well, anyhow, come over right away, Smokey, and make me an offer in cash on as much of this household stuff as you figure that you could use when you git married. O.K.?

[*He hangs up.*]

GEORGE: Hong Kong?

RALPH: Yeah.

GEORGE: Well, how about that! Back to Miss Lotus Blossom in the Pavilion of Joys?

RALPH: I never had it so good. At least not *since.*

ISABEL [*acidly*]: Mr. Bates, your character has changed since my gypsy husband appeared! He seems to have had an immediate influence on you, and not a good one. May I wash up in your bathroom?

[*They both look at her with slight, enigmatic smiles.*]

RALPH: What's that, honey?

ISABEL: Will you let me use your bathroom?

RALPH: Aw, sure, honey. I'm sorry you—

GEORGE: Now what's the matter with her?

[*He turns to* ISABEL.]

Now what's the matter with you?

ISABEL: May I talk to you alone? In another room?

RALPH: You all go in the bedroom and straighten things out.

[RALPH *goes out into the snow flurry.* GEORGE *leads* ISABEL *into next room.*]

GEORGE: Now what's the matter with you?

ISABEL: Is this a sample of how I'm going to be treated?

GEORGE: What do you mean? How have I treated you, huh?

42

ISABEL: I might as well not be present! For all the attention I have been paid since you and your buddy had this tender reunion!

GEORGE: Aren't you being a little unreasonable, honey?

ISABEL: I don't think so. George? If you are unhappy, our marriage can still be annulled. Y'know that, don't you?

GEORGE: You want to get *out* of it, do you?

[RALPH *comes back in with her traveling case. He sets it down and goes to the kitchenette.*]

ISABEL: I don't think it's really very unreasonable of me to want to be treated as if I LIVED! EXISTED!

GEORGE: Will you quit actin' like a spoiled little bitch? I want to tell you something. You're the first woman that ever put me down! Sleepin' las' night in a chair? What kind of basis is that for a happy marriage?

ISABEL: You had to get drunk on a highway! In a heaterless funeral car, after informing me you had just quit your job! Blasting my eardrums, afterward, with a car radio you wouldn't let me turn down. How was I supposed to react to such kindness? Women are human beings and I am not an exception to that rule, I assure you! I HATED YOU LAST NIGHT AFTER YOU HAD BEEN HATING ME AND TORTURING ME ALL DAY LONG!

[RALPH *comes back into the front room.*]

GEORGE: Torturing you, did you say? WHY DON'T YOU SIMMER DOWN! We ain't ALONE here, y'know!

RALPH: [*quietly, from the living room*]: You all are just goin' through a perfectly usual little period of adjustment. That's all it is, I told her—

GEORGE: Aw! You all have been talking?

ISABEL: What did you think we'd been doing while you were gone in that instrument of torture you have for a car?

GEORGE: You've got to simmer down to a lower boiling point, baby.

RALPH [*entering the bedroom*]: Just goin' through a period of adjustment. . . .

ISABEL: Adjustment to what, Mr. Bates? Humiliation? For the rest of my life? Well, I won't have it! I don't want such an "adjustment." I want to— May I—

[*She sobs.*]

—freshen up a little bit in your bathroom before we drive downtown? To check in at a hotel?

RALPH: Sure you can.

GEORGE: I ain't goin' downtown—or checkin' in no hotel.

[*He goes back into the living room.*]

ISABEL: YOU may do as you *please! I'm* checking in a hotel.

RALPH [*offering her a glass*]: You never finished your drink.

ISABEL: I don't care to, thanks. Too many people think that liquor solves problems, all problems. I think all it does is *confuse* them!

RALPH: I would say that it—*obfuscates* them a little, but—

ISABEL: Does *what* to them, Mr. Bates?

44

RALPH: I work crossword puzzles. I—ha ha!—pick up a lot of long words. Obfuscates means obscures. And problems need obfuscation now and then, honey. I don't mean total or permanent obfuscation, I just mean *temporary* obfuscation, that's all.

[*He is touched by the girl and he is standing close to her, still holding the glass out toward her. He has a fine, simple sweetness and gentleness when he's not "bugged" by people.*]

D'ya always say *Mister* to men?

ISABEL: Yes, I do till I know them. I had an old-fashioned upbringing and I can't say I regret it. Yes.

[*She is still peering out the door at her new husband.*]

RALPH: I wish you would say Ralph to me like you *know* me, honey. You got a tension between you, and tensions obfuscate love. Why don't you get that cross look off your face and give him a loving expression? Obfuscate his problems with a sweet smile on your face and—

ISABEL: YOU do that! I'm not in a mood to "obfuscate" his problems. Mr. Bates, I think he'd do better to face them like I'm facing mine, such as the problem of having married a man that seems to dislike me after one day of marriage.

RALPH: Finish this drink and obfuscate that problem because it doesn't exist.

[*He closes the bedroom door. As he comes back to Isabel with the glass,* GEORGE *reopens the door between the two rooms, glares in for a moment and switches the overhead light on, then goes back into the parlor.* RALPH *smiles tolerantly at this show of distrust which is not justified.*]

ISABEL: You have a sweet little bedroom, Mr. Bates.

45

RALPH: I married a *sweet, homely* woman. Almost started to *like* her. I can like *anybody*, but—

ISABEL: Mr. Bates? Ralph? This house has a *sweetness* about it!

RALPH: You don't think it's "tacky?"

ISABEL: No. I think it's—sweet!

RALPH: We got it cheap because this section of town is built right over a cavern.

ISABEL [*without listening*]: What?

RALPH: This High Point suburb is built over an underground cavern and is gradually sinking down in it. You see those cracks in the walls?

ISABEL: Oh. . . .

[*She hasn't listened to him or looked.*]

Oh! My little blue bag. May I have it?

RALPH [*through the door*]: She wants a little blue bag.

GEORGE: *Here, give it to her, goddam it!*

[*He tosses the bag into the bedroom.* ISABEL *screams.* RALPH *catches the bag.*]

Now whatcha screamin' faw?

ISABEL: Thank heaven Mr. Bates is such a good catch. All my colognes and perfumes are in that bag, including a twenty-five dollar bottle of Vol-de-nuit. Mr. Bates, will it be necessary for me to phone the hotel?

GEORGE: Didn't you hear what I said?

ISABEL: Mr. Bates! Would you mind phoning some clean, inexpensive hotel to hold a room for us tonight?

GEORGE: I said I'm not gonna check in a hotel tonight!

ISABEL: Reserve a *single* room, please!

RALPH: Sure, sure, honey, I'll do that. Now you just rest an' fresh up an'— Come on, George, let her alone here now, so she can rest an' calm down.

[*He leads* GEORGE *back into the parlor.*]

GEORGE: Look at my hands! Willya look at my hands?

RALPH: What about your hands?

GEORGE: Remember that tremor? Which I had in Korea? Those shakes? Which started in Korea?

RALPH: Aw is it come back on yuh?

GEORGE: Are you blind, man?

RALPH: Yeah. How's your drink?

GEORGE: She in the bathroom yet?

RALPH: Naw, she's still in the bedroom.

GEORGE: Wait'll she gits in the bathroom so we can talk.

RALPH: What's your drink, ole son?

GEORGE: Beer's fine. Jesus!

RALPH [*at the bar*]: Rough?

GEORGE: Just wait'll she gits in the bathroom so I can tell you about last night.

RALPH: Here.

[*He hands him a beer.*]

GEORGE [*at the bedroom door*]: She's still sittin' there bawling on that bed. Step outside a minute.

47

[*He goes to the front door and out onto the tiny paved porch. The interior dims as* RALPH *follows him out. For a while they just stand drinking beer with the snow shadows swarming about them.*]

RALPH: Chilly.

GEORGE: I don't feel chilly.

RALPH: *I* do.

[*He pauses.*]

You're not for that little lady in that damn silly little sissy mess of a bedroom!

GEORGE: What's wrong with the bedroom, it looked like a nice little bedroom.

RALPH: A bedroom is just as nice as whoever sleeps in it with you.

GEORGE: I missed that. What was that, now?

[*He rests an arm on Ralph's shoulders.*]

RALPH: How would you like ev'ry time you wint t'bed with your wife, you had to imagine on the bed in the dark that it wasn't her on it with you, in the dark with you, but any one of a list of a thousand or so lovely lays? I done a despicable thing. I married a girl that had no attraction for me excepting I felt sorry for her and her old man's money! I got what I should have gotten: nothing! Just a goddam desk job at Regal Dairy Products, one of her daddy's business operations in Memphis, at eighty-five lousy rutten dollars a week! With my background? In the Air Force?

GEORGE: Man an air record will cut you no ice on the ground. All it leaves you is a—mysterious tremor. Come on back in. I'm freezing to death out here. I'll git her into that bathroom so we can talk.

[*He tosses the beer cans into yard.*]

RALPH: Don't y'know better'n to throw beer cans in a man's front yard?

[*He says this vaguely, glumly, as he follows* GEORGE *back into the cottage and shuts the door behind them.* GEORGE *goes to bedroom.*]

GEORGE [*entering*]: Little Bit, you told me you couldn't wait to get under a good hot shower. There's a good shower in that bathroom. Why don't you go and get under that good hot shower?

ISABEL: I have a lot to think over, George.

GEORGE: Think it over under a good shower in that bedroom, will you? I want to take a bath, too.

ISABEL [*suddenly turning to face him from the bed*]: George, I feel so lonely!

GEORGE: Yeah, and whose fault is that?

ISABEL: I don't know why I suddenly felt so lonely!

[*She sobs again. He regards her coolly from the door.*]

GEORGE: Little Bit, go in the bathroom and take your shower, so I can go take mine, or do you want us to go in and take one together?

[*She rises with a sigh and goes to bathroom door.*]

Naw, I didn't think so.

[*She enters the bathroom. He waits till the shower starts, then returns to the front room.*]

There now, she's in!

[*He shakes both fists in the air with a grimace of torment.*]

49

Look! I got to get rid of that girl. I got to get rid of her quick. Jesus, you got to help me. I can't stay with that girl.

RALPH: Man, you're married to her.

GEORGE: You're married to one! Where's yours? You son of a tail gun! Don't tell me I'm married to her when we ain't exchanged five remarks with each other since we drove out of Cape Girardeau where she refused to—has she come out of the bathroom? No!—Even *undress!* But huddled up in a chair all night in a blanket, crying? Because she had the misfortune to be my wife?

RALPH: I wouldn't count on it.

GEORGE: On what?

RALPH: Her thinking it's such a misfortune.

GEORGE: I described to you how we passed the night, last night!

RALPH: Is this girl a virgin?

GEORGE: She is a *cast-iron* virgin! And's going to stay one! Determined!

RALPH: I wouldn't count on that.

GEORGE: I would. I count on it. First thing I do tomorrow is pack her onto a plane back to Saint Louie.

RALPH: You must have done something to shock her.

GEORGE: That's the truth, I tried to sleep with her.

RALPH: Maybe you handled the little lady too rough.

GEORGE: Now don't talk to me like a wise old man of the mountain about how to deal with a woman. Who was it had to make dates for who at Big Springs and who was it even had to make arrangements for you with those Toyko dolls?

RALPH: That's not women, that's gash.

GEORGE: Gash are women.

RALPH: They are used women. You've got a unused woman and got to approach her as one.

GEORGE: She's gonna stay unused as far as I am concerned.

[He stoops by the Christmas tree.]

Now what the hell is this thing?

[He has crouched among the toys under the tree.]

RALPH: Rocket launcher. Miniature of the rocket-launchin' pad at Cape Canaveral.

GEORGE: No snow! How's it work?

RALPH: Gimme the countdown. I'll show you.

GEORGE: Ten. Nine. Eight. Seven. Six. Five. Four. Three. Two. Oww!

[The rocket has fired in his face.]

RALPH: Ain't you got sense enough to stand clear of a rocket launcher? Ha ha! Last week, just last week, I caught the little bugger playin' with a rag doll. Well. I snatched that doll away from him an' pitched it into the fireplace. He tried to pull it out an' burned his hand! Dotty called me a monster! The child screamed "I hate you!" an' kicked my shins black an' blue! But I'll be damned if any son of Ralph Bates will grow up playin' with dolls. Why, I'll bet you he rides this hawss side-saddle! Naw, a sissy tendency in a boy's got to be nipped in the bud, otherwise the bud will blossom.

GEORGE: I would prefer to have a little girl.

[He says this wistfully, still rubbing his bruised forehead.]

Little girls prefer Daddy. Female instinct comes out early in them.

RALPH: I wanted a boy but I'm not sure I got one. However, I got him a real red-blooded boy's Christmas, at no small expense for a man in my income bracket!

[ISABEL *comes out of the bathroom.*]

I like the kid, I mean I—sure would suffer worse than he would if the neighborhood gang called him "Sissy!" I'm tolerant. By nature. But if I git partial custody of the kid, even one month in summer, I will correct the sissy tendency in him. Because in this world you got to be what your physical sex is or correct it in Denmark. I mean we got a *man's* world coming up, man! Technical! Terrific! And it's gotta be *fearless*! *Terrific*!

ISABEL: Mr. Bates.

GEORGE: [*on his way to the door*]: Whadaya want?

ISABEL: I called for Mistuh Bates.

GEORGE: Mistuh Bates, Mrs. Haverstick is anxious to talk to you, suh.

ISABEL: I just want to know if you have called the hotel.

RALPH [*entering*]: Sure, sure, honey. Don't worry about a thing. Everything's gonna be fine.

ISABEL: [*she is in a silk robe*]: Thanks, Ralph. You've been awf'ly kind to me. Oh! I helped myself to a little Pepto-Bismol I found in your sweet little bathroom.

RALPH: Aw, that pink stuff? Take it all. I never touch it. It's Dorothea's. She used to get acid stomach.

ISABEL: It's very soothing.

52

[GEORGE *crosses to the bedroom door, head cocked, somewhat suspicious.*]

RALPH: Well, I cured her of that. I doubt that she's hit that Pepto-Bismol bottle once in the last five years.

ISABEL: I rarely suffer from an upset stomach. Rarely as snow in Memphis!

[*She laughs lightly.*]

But the human stomach is an emotional barometer with some people. Some get headaches, others get upset stomachs.

RALPH: Some even git diarrhea.

ISABEL: The combination of nervous strain and— Oh! What's this?

[*She picks up a gorgeously robed statue of the infant Jesus.*]

RALPH: Aw, that.

[*He moves farther into the bedroom.* GEORGE *moves closer to the door.*]

That's the infant of Prague. Prague, Czechoslovakia?

ISABEL: Oh?

RALPH: It was discovered there in the ruins of an old monastery. It has miraculous properties.

ISABEL: Does it?

RALPH: They say that it does. Whoever gives you the Infant of Prague gives you a piece of money to put underneath it for luck. Her father presented this infant to Dorothea so the piece of money was *naturally one penny.* It's s'posed to give you prosperity if you're not prosperous and a child if you're childless. It give us a child but the money is yet to

53

come in, the money's just been goin' out. However, I don't blame the Infant of Prague for that, because—

ISABEL: Mr. Bates? Ralph? You know, very often people can be absolutely blind, stupid, and helpless about their own problems and still have a keen intuition about the problems of others?

RALPH: Yeah?

ISABEL: There is such a tender atmosphere in this sweet little house, especially this little bedroom, you can almost— touch it, feel it! I mean you can *breathe* the tender atmosphere in it!

RALPH [*in a slow, sad drawl*]: The color scheme in this bedroom is battleship gray. And will you notice the cute inscriptions on the twin beds? "His" on this one, "Hers" on that one? The linen's marked his and hers, too. Well. The space between the two beds was no-man's land for a while. Her psychological frigidity was like a, like a—artillery barrage!—between his and hers. I didn't try to break through it the first few nights. Nope. I said to myself, "Let *her* make the first move."

ISABEL: *Did* she?

RALPH: What do *you* think?

ISABEL: I think she *did*.

RALPH: *Right you are!*

[*He gives her a little congratulatory pat on the shoulder.*]

GEORGE: What's this heart-to-heart talk goin' on in here?

RALPH [*chuckling*]: Come on out of here, boy. I got something to tell you.

[*He leads* GEORGE *out.*]

54

GEORGE: What were you up to in there?

RALPH: [*whispering loudly*]: Go in there, quick, before she gets dressed, you fool!

GEORGE: I'll be damned if I will!

RALPH: I'll turn the TV on loud.

ISABEL [*calling out*]: I'll be dressed in a jiffy!

RALPH: Go ON! You just got a jiffy!

GEORGE: Yeah, and I've got some pride, too. She put me down last night, first woman ever to put me down in—

RALPH: I know, you told me, GO IN! Lock the door and—

GEORGE: YOU go in! That's what you WANT to do! I never had a girl yet that you didn't want to take over. This time you're welcome. GO IN! GO BACK IN AND BREATHE THE TENDER ATMOSPHERE OF THAT—

RALPH: Gawge? Hey—You're *shakin'*, man, you're shakin' to pieces! What kind of a son of a bitch d'you take me faw?

GEORGE: The kind which you are, which you always have been!

RALPH: She is right about you. You are not well, son. . . .

GEORGE: Where d'ya git this "son" stuff! Don't call me "son."

RALPH: Then grow up, will yuh! What's your drink? Same?

GEORGE: Same . . .

RALPH: You're shakin' because you want to go in that bedroom. GO IN! Take the bottle in with you! I'll sit here and watch TV till—

[ISABEL *has put on her traveling suit. She comes into the living room.*]

—Too late *now*!

ISABEL [*in a sweet Texas drawl*]: Mr. Bates? Ralph? It breaks my heart to see all those lovely child's toys under the tree and the little boy not here to have his Christmas.

RALPH: He's with his mother.

ISABEL: I know, but his Christmas is here.

RALPH: He's a Mama's boy. He's better off with his Mama.

ISABEL: How are *you* feeling, now, George?

[GEORGE *grunts and turns to the bar.*

[ISABEL *makes a despairing gesture to Ralph.*

[GEORGE *wheels about abruptly, suspecting some dumb-play.*

[ISABEL *laughs lightly and then sighs deeply.*]

GEORGE: I thought you'd set your heart on a single hotel room tonight.

ISABEL: George, you're shaking worse than I've even seen you.

GEORGE: That's, that's not your problem, that's—*my* problem, not *yours!*

RALPH: [*to Isabel*]: Honey? Come here a minute.

[*He whispers something to her.*]

ISABEL: Oh, no. No! Mr. Bates, you are confusing the function of a wife with that of a— I feel sorry, I feel very sorry for you not-so-young young men who've depended for love, for tenderness in your lives, on the sort of women available near army camps, in occupied territories! Mr. Bates? Ralph?

56

RALPH: Just take his hand and lead him into the—

ISABEL: RALPH! NO! BELIEVE ME!

RALPH: All right. . . .

[*There is a pause.*]

ISABEL: Ralph, why did you quit YOUR job? Did you get the shakes, too?

GEORGE: Don't get bitchy with him.

ISABEL: I WASN'T BEING BITCHY!

RALPH: She wasn't being bitchy. She asked a logical question.

ISABEL: Just a question!

GEORGE: Can't you mind your own business for a change? You got fired too, don't forget! All three of us here is jobless!

ISABEL: I am not forgetting.

[*Primly, with dignity.*]

I am not forgetting a thing, and I have a lot to remember.

GEORGE: Good. I hope you remember it. *Memorize* it!

[*He is getting tight.*]

ISABEL [*sniffling a little*]: I think I caught cold in that car.

GEORGE: Hell, you were born with a cold—

ISABEL: *Stop that*!

GEORGE: In your damn little—

ISABEL: MR. BATES, MAKE HIM STOP!

RALPH: Let him blow off some steam.

[Overlapping barely intelligible]

57

GEORGE: Incurable cold! You didn't catch it from me.

ISABEL: I wish you had shown this side of your nature before, just a hint, just a clue, so I'd have known what I was in for.

GEORGE: What hint did you give *me*? What clue did *I* have to *your* nature?

ISABEL: Did I disguise my nature?

GEORGE: You sure in hell did.

ISABEL: In what *way,* tell me, please!

GEORGE: You didn't put the freeze on me at Barnes Hospital!

[*To Ralph.*]

She was nurse at Barnes when I went there for those tests? To find out the cause of my shakes? She was my night nurse at Barnes.

ISABEL: Oh, stop! Don't be so crude! How can you be so crude?

GEORGE: She was my night nurse at Barnes and gave me alcohol rubdowns at bedtime.

ISABEL: That was my job. I had to.

GEORGE: Hell, she stroked and petted me with her hands like she had on a pair of silk gloves.

ISABEL: This is insufferable. I am going downtown.

[*She covers her face, sobbing.*]

Just give me carfare downtown.

GEORGE: You remember those dolls with silk gloves on their hands in Tokyo, Ralph? Hell, she could of given them Jap dolls lessons!

ISABEL: I DID NOT TOUCH YOUR BODY EXCEPT AS A NURSE HIRED TO DO IT! YOU KNOW I DIDN'T! I DID NOT TOUCH YOUR BIG OLD LECHEROUS BODY.

GEORGE: How'd you give me a rubdown without touching my body? Huh? How could you give me rubdowns without touching my body? Huh?

ISABEL: Please, please, make him be still. Mr. Bates? You believe me? He's making out I seduced him while I was his nurse.

GEORGE: I didn't say that. Don't say I said that. I didn't say that. I said you had soft little fingers and you knew what you were doing. She'd say, "Turn over." I couldn't turn over. I had to stay on my stomach. I was embarrassed not to.

ISABEL: Ah—I feel nauseated. What filth you have in your mind!

RALPH: Honey? Little lady? Come over and sit here with me. All this will all straighten out. It's going to be all straightened out.

[GEORGE *pours himself a drink. The glass slips out of his shaking fingers.*]

GEORGE: *Worse than ever, worse than ever before!* How could I have kept that job? A ground mechanic with hands that can't hold tools?

ISABEL: Go take your tranquillizers. They're in my zipper bag.

GEORGE: Oh, Jesus.

RALPH [*picking up the dropped glass*]: See, honey? That boy isn't well. Make some allowances for him. You're both nice kids, both of you, wonderful people. And very good-looking people. I'm afraid you're doomed to be happy for a

59

long time together, soon as this little period of adjustment that you're going through right now passes over.

[GEORGE *holds his violently shaking hands in front of him, staring at them fiercely.*

[*He goes to the bedroom.*]

May I call my father, collect?

RALPH: Don't call home, now. Why upset the old people on Christmas Eve?

ISABEL: I'll just say I miss them and want to come home for Christmas.

RALPH: They'll know something's wrong if you go home without your brand-new husband.

ISABEL: Husband! What husband? That man who describes me as a Tokyo whore? Implies that I seduced him in a hospital because I was required to give him alcohol rubdowns at night?

RALPH: All he meant was you excited him, honey.

ISABEL: I assure you that was *not* my intention! I am naturally gentle, I am gentle by nature, and if my touch on his big lecherous body created—*sexual fantasies* in his *mind*! —that's hardly *my* fault, is it?

GEORGE [*returning*]: I am sorry that I upset you.

ISABEL: Will you tell him the truth?

GEORGE: Sure I will. What about?

ISABEL: Did I deliberately excite you in Barnes Hospital?

GEORGE: No. I never said that.

ISABEL: Anybody that heard you would get that impression.

60

GEORGE: You didn't deliberately do it, you just did it because I was horny for you, that's all, that's all, that's—all. . . .

[*He slumps in a chair with a long, despairing sigh.*

[*There is a silent pause.*]

ISABEL: I don't blame you alone, George. I blame myself, too. Not for deliberate sexual provocation, but for not realizing before our marriage yesterday that we were—opposite types.

GEORGE [*sadly*]: Yes, opposite types. . . .

ISABEL: *I want to talk to my father*!

GEORGE: Talk to him. Call him. I'll pay Ralph the charges.

ISABEL: May I?

RALPH: Sure, honey, call your folks and wish 'em a Merry Christmas.

ISABEL: Thank you. I will if I can stop crying.

RALPH: George? This little girl needs you. Go on, be nice to her, boy.

GEORGE: I need somebody, too. She hasn't got the incurable shakes, *I* have, *I* got 'em! Was *she* nice to *me*? *Last night*?

ISABEL [*tearfully*]: Operator? I want to call long distance, Sweetwater, Texas. Oh-seven-oh-three. No, anybody that answers. It will be Daddy, Mama can't get out of—

[*She sobs.*]

—bed!

[RALPH *makes a sign to George to go over and sit by her.*

GEORGE *disregards the suggestion.*]

61

RALPH: You better hang up and let them call you back. Long distance is very busy on Christmas Eve. Everyone callin' the home folks.

ISABEL: I just hope I stop crying! I don't want Daddy to hear me.

[*She pauses.*]

Poor ole thing. So sweet and faithful to Mama, bedridden with arthritis for seven years, now . . . Hello? What? Oh. You'll call me back when you complete the connection, will you, because it's very important, it's really very urgent. . . .

[*She hangs up. There is silence.*]

RALPH [*finally*]: One bad night in a rutten highway motel and you all are acting like born enemies toward each other!

GEORGE: Don't upset her, she's going to talk to her daddy. And tell him she's married to a stinker.

ISABEL: No, I'm not. I'm going to tell him that I am blissfully happy, married to the kindest man in the world, the second kindest, the kindest man next to my daddy!

GEORGE: Thanks.

ISABEL: Waits hand and foot on Mama, bedridden with arthritis.

GEORGE: You told Ralph about that.

ISABEL: And has held down a job in a pharmacy all these years. . . .

GEORGE: Wonderful. I didn't expect to marry a girl in love with her father.

ISABEL: George Haverstick, you are truly a monster!

[*The phone rings.*

[*She snatches it up.*]

What?—DAD! OH, PRECIOUS DADDY!

[*She bursts into violent tears.*]

Can't talk, can't talk, can't talk, can't talk, *can't—talk*!

RALPH: Honey, gi' me the phone!

[*She surrenders it to him.*]

Hello? Hi, Pop, merry Christmas. No, this isn't George, this is a buddy of his. Isabel wants to talk to you to tell you how happy she is, but she just broke up with emotion. You know how it is, don't you, Pop? Newlyweds? They're naturally full of emotion. They got to go through a little period of adjustment between them.——Fine, yes, she's fine. She'll talk to you soon as she blows her nose. Hey, honey? Your daddy wants to talk to you.

[*She takes the phone, then bursts into violent sobbing again, covering her mouth and handing the phone back to* RALPH.]

Pop? I'll have to talk for her. She's all shook up.

[*He forces the phone back into* ISABEL'S *hand.*]

ISABEL [*choked.*] Dad?

[*She bawls again, covering the mouthpiece.* RALPH *takes the phone back from her.*]

RALPH: Pop? Just talk to her, Pop. She's too shook up to talk back.

[*He forces the phone into her hands again.*]

ISABEL: Dad? How are you, Daddy? Are you? That's wonderful, Daddy. Oh, I'm fine, too. I got married yesterday.

63

Yesterday . . . How is Mom? Just the same? Daddy? I may be seeing you soon. Yes. You know I gave up my nursing job at Barnes when I married and so I have lots of free time and I might just suddenly pop in on you—*tomorrow*!——I love you and miss you so much! Good-by, Merry Christmas, Daddy!

[*She hangs up blindly and goes over to the Christmas tree.*]

I think it's awful your little boy's missing his Christmas. Such a wonderful Christmas. A choo-choo train with depot and tunnel, cowboy outfit, chemical set and a set of alphabet blocks. . . .

GEORGE: He knows what he got for his kid, you don't have to tell him.

[*There is a pause.*]

ISABEL: Well, now, I feel better, after talking to Daddy.

GEORGE: Does it make you feel uplifted, spiritually?

ISABEL: I feel less lonely. That's all.

GEORGE: I wonder if it would have that effect on me if I called my daddy or mama in Amarillo? That's in Texas, too. Maybe I'd feel less lonely. Huh, Little Bit?

[*She starts out.*]

Just wait a minute. I want to tell you something. In my thirty-four years I've been with a fair share of women and you are the first, you are the first of the lot, that has found me repulsive.

ISABEL: I don't find you "repulsive," not even your vanity, George, silly but not repulsive.

RALPH: Hey, now, you all quit this.

64

GEORGE: Can you stand there and tell me you find me attractive?

ISABEL: I'm afraid I can't, at this moment.

GEORGE: Well, goddam it, what in hell did you marry me faw?

ISABEL: Mr. Bates, your animal is standing by the door as as if it wants out. Shall I let it out for you?

RALPH: You two are just goin' through this adjustment period that all young couples go through.

ISABEL: Such a sweet animal! What is this animal's name?

GEORGE: The animal is a dog.

ISABEL: I know it's a dog.

GEORGE: Then why don't you call it a dog!

RALPH: Better put 'er lead on 'er. Her name is Bess.

ISABEL: Shall we take a walk, Bessie? Huh? A nice little run in the snow. See! She does want out. Oh! My coat. . . .

RALPH: Here, put on this one, honey.

[*He takes the beaver coat out of the Christmas box under the tree.*]

ISABEL: Oh, what beautiful sheared beaver! It's your wife's Christmas present?

RALPH: It was but it ain't no more.

ISABEL: How soft! Now I know that you love her. You couldn't feel the softness of this fur and not know it was bought as a present for someone you love.

RALPH: Put it on. It's yours. A wedding present to you.

65

ISABEL: Oh, no I—

RALPH: WILL YOU PLEASE PUT IT ON YUH?

ISABEL: I guess the snow won't hurt it. Come on, Bessie, that's a good lady, come on. . . .

[*She goes out.*]

GEORGE: I know of *two* animals that want out and one of them ain't no dawg!

ISABEL [*returning*]: I heard you say that!

GEORGE: Well, good.

ISABEL: If you want out of our marriage, a divorce isn't necessary. We can just get an annulment! So maybe last night was fortunate after all!

[*She stares at him a moment and then goes back out with the dog. As they leave, the dog is barking at something outside.*

[GEORGE *comes up beside Ralph and rests an affectionate arm on his shoulders.*

[*The tempo now becomes very fast.*]

RALPH: You old Texas jack rabbit!

GEORGE: You tail-gunner son of a—How you feel?

RALPH: I feel fine!

[*They chuckle shyly together. Then:*

[*They catch each other in an affectionate bear hug.*]

GEORGE: How much money you got?

RALPH: Why?

GEORGE: Remember how we talked about going into something together when we got out of the service? Well, we're out of the service. How much money do you think you can raise?

RALPH: What are *your* assets, Buddy?

GEORGE: I've saved five hundred dollars and can get a thousand for that '52 Caddy.

RALPH: You can't go into no business on as little as that.

GEORGE: You're selling out this house and everything in it, ain't you?

RALPH: I'd have to split it with Dorothea, I reckon.

GEORGE: Look. Let's cut out tomorrow. Let's go to Texas together. We can swing the financing to pick up a piece of ranchland near San Antone and raise us a herd of fine cattle.

RALPH: Why San Antone?

GEORGE: I said near it. It's a beautiful town. A winding river goes through it.

RALPH: Uh-huh. You mentioned "swing the financing." How did you—visualize—that?

GEORGE: Noticed my car out there?

RALPH: That funeral limousine?

GEORGE: We cut out of here tomorrow bright and early and drive straight through to West Texas. In West Texas we git us a colored boy, put a showfer's cap on him an' set him back of the wheel. He drives us up in front of the biggest San Antone bank and there we demand an immediate interview with the president of it. My folks staked out West Texas. The name of the first George Haverstick in West Texas is engraved on the memorial tablet to the Alamo heroes in San

67

Antone! I'm not snowin' you, man! An' they's no better credit card in West Texas than an ancestor's name on that memorial tablet. We will arrive at lunch time an'—invite this bank executive to lunch at the San Antone country club to which I can git us a guest card an' befo' we're in sight of the golf links the financing deal will be swung!

RALPH: Man, a bank president has rode in a awful lot of funeral processions. It's almost one of his main professional duties. He's rode in too many funeral limousines not to know when he's in one. And ain't you afraid that he might, well— notice your shakes?

GEORGE: This little tremor would disappear completely the moment I crossed into Texas!

RALPH: I hope so, man, permanently and completely, but—

GEORGE: Go on. Tear down the project!

RALPH: There's no Ralph Bates, first, second, third, fourth or fifth on that memorial tablet to those—Alamo heroes.

GEORGE: Haven't you blazoned your name in the memory of two wars?

RALPH: Who remembers two wars? Or even one, after some years. There's a great public amnesia about a former war hero.

[*He goes reflectively to the front door.*]

GEORGE: Where you goin'?

RALPH: I'm goin' out to think in this cool night air.

[*He exits onto the paved terrace, switching off the interior lights.* GEORGE *follows gravely.* RALPH *stoops to light up a string of colored bulbs that cover the arched entrance to carport.*

68

[*It casts a dim rainbow glow on the terrace. Shadowy flakes of snow drift through it.*]

Why San Antone? Why cattle? Why not electric equipment?

GEORGE: I know San Antone and cattle!

RALPH: And I know electric equipment.

GEORGE: Yes, you can turn on a set of little Christmas tree lights.

RALPH: I don't want to be your ranch hand!

GEORGE: We'd buy in *equal*.

RALPH: How? One minute you say you'll liquidate all your assets that only appear to be an old funeral car, the next you say we'll drive a bank president out in this funeral car, and you want me to put up all that I realize on the sale of this property here? Your sense of equity is very unequal, and shit-fire anyhow, even if I sell this property, by remote control, from Hong Kong, and Dotty's folks would sure in hell block the transaction—well, look at the cracks in this stucco, y'know how they got there? This Goddam High Point suburb —*listen!*—happens to be built over a great big underground cavern into which it is *sinking!*

GEORGE: *Sinking?*

RALPH: I'm not snowing you, man, this whole community here is gradually sinking, inch by inch by year, into this subterranean cavern and the property owners and the real-estate promoters are in collusion to keep this secret about it: so we can sell out to the next bunch of suckers: DISGUSTING!

GEORGE: Built over a—

RALPH: *Cavern: yes!*—a *big subterranean cavern*, but so is *your* project, not to mention your *marriage. Cattle!—Cattle?*

GEORGE: The Texas Longhorn isn't just cattle, it's a—dignified beast.

RALPH: Did you say Texas Longhorn? Son, the Texas Longhorn is not only dignified, it is *obsolete.*

GEORGE: Historical, yeah, like the Haversticks of West Texas.

RALPH: The Haversticks of West Texas are not yet obsolete, are they?

GEORGE: I am the last one of 'em an' the prospects of another don't look bright at this moment. But the Texas Longhorn—

[*He exhales.*]

—compared to modern beef cattle such as your Hereford or your Black Angus—it has no carcass value.

RALPH: Well, in that case, why don't you *breed* the Black Angus or the—

GEORGE: I anticipated that question.

RALPH: I hope you're prepared with some answer. . . .

GEORGE [*draws on cigarette and flips it away*]: Le' me put it this way. How would you like to breed a herd of noble cattle, a herd that stood for the frontier days of this country!—an' ride to the depot one mawnin' in your station wagon, the name of your ranch stamped on it, to watch these great, dignified beasts being herded onto a string of flatcars, penned in and hauled off to K City packin' houses, Chicago slaughterhouses, the shockin' atrocities which cannot even be thought about without a shudder!—an' wave 'em good-by as if they was off for a mother-lovin' church picnic?

RALPH: It's it's a—heart-breakin' pitcher!

[*He chuckles.*]

But I do love a good steak, ha ha! A prime-cut sirloin, however— What would you want to breed this noble herd for? For *kicks*, for—?

GEORGE: *You* got TV in there, ain't you? Turn on your TV any late afternoon or early evenin' and what do you get— beside the commercials, I mean? A goddam Western, on film. Y'know what I see, outside the camera range? A big painted sign that says: "Haverstick-Bates Ranch"—or "Bates-Haverstick," you can have top billing!—"The Last Stand of the Texas Longhorn, a Dignified Beast! We breed cattle for TV Westerns." We breed us some buffalo, too. The buffalo is also a dignified beast, almost extinct, only thirty thousand head of the buffalo left in this land. We'll increase that number by a sizable fraction. Hell, we could double that number befo' we—

RALPH: Hang up our boots an' saddles under the—dignified sky of West Texas?

GEORGE [*with feeling*]: There *is* dignity in that sky! There's dignity in the agrarian, the pastoral—way of—existence! A dignity too long lost out of the—American dream—

[*He is shaking a good deal with emotion.*]

—as it used to be in the West Texas-Haverstick days. . . .

RALPH: But I want to be dignified, too.

GEORGE: Human dignity's what I'm—

RALPH: I don't want to be caught short by a Texas Longhorn while crossing a pasture one mawnin' in West Texas! Ha ha ha. Naw, I don't want to catch me an ass full of Texas Longhorns before I can jump a fence rail out of that West Texas pasture. I—

GEORGE: SHUT UP! WILL YUH? YOU TV WATCHIN', CANNED-BEER DRINKIN', SPANISH-SUBURBAN-STUCCO-TYPE SON OF—Y'KNOW I THINK BEER IS DOPED? DOPED? I THINK THEY DOPE IT TO CREATE A NATIONAL TOLERANCE OF THE TV COMMERCIAL! No—No—I'm sorry I come through Dixon. . . .

[He moves away, sadly.]

I cherished a memory of you—

*[*CAROLERS *are heard from a distance.]*

—idolized an old picture of which I was suddenly faced with a, with a—*goddam travesty* of it!—When you opened the door and I was confronted with a —DEFEATED! MIDDLE-AGED! NEGATIVE! LOST!—poor bastard . . .

RALPH: What do you think I saw when I opened that door? A ghostly apparition!

GEORGE: ME?

RALPH: A young man I used to know with an old man's affliction: the palsy!

GEORGE: Thanks!—I appreciate that.

[Next door the CAROLERS *sing: "God Rest Ye Merry, Gentlemen, May Nothing Ye Dismay!"]*

Oh, man, oh brother, I sure do appreciate that!

[He sits down quickly, shaking fiercely, in a metal porch chair, turning it away from Ralph to face the audience. RALPH *is immediately and truly contrite.]*

Yeah. In addition to those other changes I mentioned in you, you've now exposed another which is the worst of the bunch. You've turned *vicious!*

RALPH: Aw, now—

72

GEORGE: Yeah, yeah, bitter and vicious! To ridicule an affliction like *mine*, like *this*, is vicious, *vicious!*

[He holds up his shaky hand. RALPH *reaches his hand out to take it but doesn't. Instead he drops his hand on George's shoulder.]*

Take that mother-grabbin' hand off my shoulder or I'll break it off you!

RALPH: You ridiculed *my* afflictions.

GEORGE: What afflictions?

RALPH: My life has been an affliction.

[He says this without self-pity, simply as a matter of fact.]

GEORGE: Now don't make me cry into this can of Budweiser with that sad, sad story of your childhood in that home for illegitimate orphans.

RALPH: *Foundlings!* Home. I was not illegitimate.

GEORGE: Foundlings are illegitimate.

RALPH: Not—*necessarily—always . . .*

[He says this with a humility that might be touching to anyone less absorbed in his own problems than George. RALPH *looks up at the drift of snow from the dark.]*

No, I meant to live a life in a Spanish-type stucco cottage in a—high point over a cavern, that is an affliction for someone that wanted and dreamed of—*oh, I wish I could be the first man in a moon rocket!* No, not the moon, but Mars, Venus! Hell, I'd like to be transported and transplanted to colonize and fertilize, to be the Adam on a—star in a different *galaxy*, yeah, that far away even!—it's wonderful knowing that such a thing is no longer inconceivable, huh?

73

GEORGE: You're talking out of character. You're a dedicated conformist, the most earthbound earth man on earth.

RALPH: If you think that about me, you never known me.

GEORGE [*starts off the terrace*]: I'm going walking, alone!

[*He stops abruptly.*]

Naw, if she sees me walking, she'll think I'm out looking for her.

RALPH: Goddam it, why don't you? Intercept her and don't say a word, just stick your hand inside that beaver-skin coat I give her and apply a little soft pressure to her—solar plexus—putting your other arm around her waist, and bring her back here, gently. . . .

GEORGE: That's what *you* want to do. Go on, *you* intercept her! And bring her back here gently!

RALPH: O.K., I *would* like to do it. But do you think I'd *do* it?

GEORGE: Can you honestly say you wouldn't put the make on her if you thought she'd give in?

RALPH: Nope! I wouldn't do it. And if you don't believe me, git back in that funeral hack and drive to West Texas in it, you—*legitimate* bastard.

GEORGE: Nope, I don't think you would. You're too much of a square.

RALPH: *There's her! There she is!*

GEORGE: Where?

RALPH: Corner. Why's she turning around? She must be lost, go get her. Look. She's joining the carolers!

GEORGE: Good, let her stay with them, and sing! Carols!

RALPH: Naw, I better go get her.

GEORGE: Go and get your *own* wife: leave mine alone!

[RALPH *puts his arm around George's shoulder.*]

And I told you to keep your rutten hand off my shoulder.

RALPH: Break it off me.

GEORGE: What I mean is, the point is—you *chose* your afflictions! Married into them. Mine I didn't choose! It just come on me, mysteriously: my shakes. You wouldn't even be interested in the awful implications of an affliction like mine.

[*He holds up his shaking hand.*]

RALPH: Sure, I'm interested in it, but—

GEORGE: S'pose it never lets up? This thing they can't treat or even find the cause of! S'pose I shake all my life like, like —dice in a crap shooter's fist?—Huh?—I mean at all moments of tension, all times of crisis, I shake! . . . Huh? And there's other aspects to it beside the career side. It could affect my love life. Huh? I could start shaking so hard when I started to make out with a girl that I couldn't do it. You know? Couldn't make the scene with her. . . .

[*There is a slight pause.*]

RALPH: Aw. Was that it?

GEORGE: Was what what?

RALPH: Was that the trouble at the Old Man River Motel, last night, you were scared of impotence with her? Was that the problem?

GEORGE: I don't have that problem. I *never* had that problem.

RALPH: No?

GEORGE: *No!*

[*Tense pause.*]

WHY? Do *you* have that problem?

RALPH: Sometimes. I wasn't excited enough by Dotty to satisfy her, sometimes. . . .

GEORGE: The thought of her old man's money couldn't always excite you?

RALPH: Nope, it couldn't always, that's the truth.

[*He switches off the lights, senselessly, and switches them back on again.*]

Poor ole Dotty. She's got so she always wants it and when I can't give it to her I feel guilty, guilty. . . .

[*He turns the Christmas lights off again, turns them back on again.*]

GEORGE: Well, you know *me*. An Eveready battery, built-in in me.

RALPH [*turning to him with a slow, gentle smile*]: Yeah, I understand, son.

GEORGE: *Don't be so damned understanding!*

RALPH: Well, there she goes—Mrs. George Haverstick the Fifth. Look. She's going up to the wrong Spanish-type stucco cottage, there's five almost identical ones in this block.

GEORGE: Don't your dawg know where it lives?

RALPH: Aw, it's a dignified beast. A constant Frigidaire pointer. Points at the Westinghouse Frij an' whines for a handout whenever you enter the kitchen. Knows everyone on the block an' pays calls like a new preacher wherever he thinks—

[*Whistles at dog*]

—he might be offered a—

[*Whistles*]

—handout.

[VOICES *down the block, hearty, drunken.*]

You better go git your wife. That Spanish-type stucco cottage is occupied by a bachelor decorator and you know how they destroy wimmen. . . . He is running a sort of a unofficial USO at his house. Service men congregate there.

GEORGE: HAH!

[*He is amused by the picture.*]

RALPH: I got to climb back in a back window because you shut this door and I had put the catch on it.

[*He crosses out the door to the carport as* GEORGE *gazes gravely off.*
The CAROLERS *are closer. They go into "God Rest Ye Merry, Gentlemen" again.*
GEORGE *is not inclined to be merry. He glares into the starless air.*
In the bedroom, a windowpane is smashed and RALPH'S *arm reaches through, his fingers groping for the window latch. He finds it, gets the window up and clambers through with some muttered invectives against the hostility of the inanimate objects of the world. As soon as he enters the interior, light and sound inside are brought up. Oddly enough, a TV Western is in progress, approaching the climax of an Indian attack or a cattle stampede. It catches* RALPH'S *attention. He turns gravely to the TV set, for the moment forgetting George outside. Gunfire subsides and the dialogue is brought up loud:*]

77

DIALOGUE

—Save your ammunition, they'll come back.

—HOW LONG HAVE WE GOT?

—Till sundown. They'll hit us again after dark.

—Let's make a run for it now!

—We'll have to abandon the wagons if we make a run for it. The Rio Grande is at least five miles south of here.

—Mount the women, one woman behind each man on the hawses, unhitch the hawses! Then stampede the cattle. That'll give us a cover while we make our break.

—What is our chances, you think?

—You want a *honest* answer or a *comforting* answer?

—Give me the honest answer.

—The comforting answer would have been fifty-fifty: I'll leave you to imagine the honest answer.

—Rosemary? Come here, a minute. Take this pistol. There's five shots in it. Save the fifth shot for yourself. Now git on this hawss behind me.

—Oh, Buck! I'm so scared!

—*Git up!* O.K. sweetheart?

—Yes!

—Hold onto me tight. Dusty, when I count ten, start the cattle stampede.

[*He starts counting, slowly.*]

GEORGE [*to himself as he paces the terrace*]: Now I don't even want her. If she asked me for it, I wouldn't give it to her, the way I feel now.

[*Sneezes.*]

Catchin' a cold out here! What's he doing in there, the motherless bastard? BATES! REMEMBER ME?

RALPH [*opening the door*]: I thought you'd gone faw your wife.

[RALPH *chuckles and holds the front door open as* GEORGE *withdraws his head from the window and reappears a moment later on the terrace.*

[RALPH *lets him in.*]

GEORGE: Will you look at that? A Western on Christmas eve, even! It's a goddam NATIONAL OBSESSIONAL.

RALPH: Yep, a national homesickness in the American heart for the old wild frontiers with the yelping redskins and the covered wagons on fire and—

GEORGE: Will you look at those miserable shorthorn cattle! Those cows, in this corny Western?

[*They both face the TV. There is a pause.*]

RALPH: Yep—an undignified beast. Man? Buddy? I don't have too much confidence in the project of the Dignified West Texas Longhorn Ranch, even now, but I will go along with you. Don't ask me why. I couldn't tell you why, but I will go along with you. Want to shake on it, Buddy?

GEORGE: That champagne ought to be cold now, let's break out that champagne now.

RALPH: It'll be still colder when you've picked up your wife.

GEORGE: I told you my policy, don't interfere with it, huh?

RALPH: Women are vulnerable creatures.

GEORGE: So's a man.

RALPH [*crosses to the kitchenette door*]: I'll open up the champagne while you pick up your wife.

GEORGE: Ralpho? Man?

RALPH: Huh?

79

GEORGE: Now I know why I come here. You're a *decent!* *square!*

[*The kitchen door swings closed on them;* CAROLERS *are singing out front. After a moment* ISABEL *appears before the house with the dog.*

[*A* LADY CAROLER *appears on the terrace with a collection plate.*]

ISABEL: Oh—I'm afraid I don't have any money to give you, but—

[*She knocks at the door.*]

Wait!—till they answer the door, I—

[*Raucous voices are heard within.*]

—Some people regard the celebration of the birthday of Jesus as a, as a—sort of a—occasion, excuse for!—just getting drunk and—*disgusting!* I'll probably have to go round the back to get in. . . .

[*Great howls of hilarity have been coming from the back of the cottage, drowning out* ISABEL's *efforts to draw attention to the front door.*]

I'm very sorry, I just don't have any money.

[*The* CAROLER *accepts this in good grace and leaves.*

[ISABEL *goes around through the carport. A few seconds later* GEORGE, *in a state of Wild West exuberance, comes charging out of the kitchen with the champagne bottle, shouting:*]

GEORGE: POWDER RIVER, POWWWWW-der RIV-errrr!—a mile wide and—

RALPH: TWO INCHES DEEP!

[He follows him out as ISABEL'*s head appears through the open window in the dim bedroom: she lifts the dog through and hoists herself over the sill.]*

GEORGE: Git me a pitcher with ice and two cans of that Ballantine's ale and I will make us BLACK VELVET!

RALPH: Huh?

GEORGE: Man, you know Black Velvet!

[He is back in the kitchen.]

I made it that time in Hong Kong when we had those girls from the—

*[*RALPH *has gone in behind him. The door swings shut as* ISABEL *picks up the bedside phone in the bedroom.]*

ISABEL: Operator? I want a cab right away, it's an *emergency, yaiss!*

[Slight pause.]

Yellow Cab? Checkered! Well, please send a cab right away to— Oh, my goodness, I can't tell you the address, oh, I'll—I'll find out the address and I'll call you right back, right away. . . .

[She hangs up with a little stricken cry, followed by convulsive sobs that she stifles forcibly. On the bed, in the pink-shaded lamplight, she looks like a little girl making a first discovery of life's sorrow. Instinctively she reaches out for the Infant of Prague; at the same time, the CAROLERS *start singing below the terrace: "I Wonder as I Wander." This is a sentimental moment, but not "sticky."]*

81

Little Boy Jesus, so lonesome on your birthday. I know how you feel, *exactly!*—

[*She clasps the infant to her breast, tenderly.*]

—just exactly, because I feel the same way. . . .

DIM OUT

INTERMISSION

No time lapse.

The men return with an open, foaming bottle of champagne, and pass it back and forth between them before the fireplace, not noticing that the dog has returned or suspecting Isabel's presence in the bedroom.

GEORGE: I put them in five categories. Those that worship it, those that love it, those that just like it, those that don't like it, those that just tolerate it, those that *don't* tolerate it, those that can't stand it, and, finally, those that not only can't stand it but want to cut it off you.

RALPH [*following him with glasses, chuckling*]: That's more than five categories.

GEORGE: How many did I name?

RALPH: I don't know. I lost count.

GEORGE: Well, you know what I mean. And I have married into that last category. What scares me is that she has had hospital training and is probably able to do a pretty good cutting job. You know what I mean?

RALPH: Ha ha, yeah. Wel-l-l. . . .

[*He sets the glasses down and takes the bottle from GEORGE. The little parlor is flickering with firelight.*]

GEORGE: Which class did you marry into? Into the same category?

RALPH: No. She got to like it. More than I did even.

GEORGE: Now you're braggin'.

RALPH: Love is a very difficult—occupation. You got to work at it, man. It ain't a thing every Tom, Dick and Harry has got a true aptitude for. Y'know what I mean? Not every Tom, Dick or Harry understands how to use it. It's not a— offensive weapon. It shouldn't be used like one. Too many guys, they use it like a offensive weapon to beat down a woman with. All right. That rouses resistance. Because a woman has pride, even a woman has pride and resents being raped, and most love-making is rape with these self-regarded —experts! That come downstairs yelling, "Oh, man, Oh, brother," and hitching their belts up like they'd accomplished something.

GEORGE [*getting the allusion and resentful*]: You mean me?

RALPH: Naw, naw, will yuh listen a minute? I've got ideas on this subject.

GEORGE: A self-regarded expert!

RALPH: You know Goddam right I'm an expert. I know I never had your good looks but made out better.

GEORGE: One man's opinion!

RALPH: Look! Lissen! You got to use—TENDERNESS! —with it, not roughness like raping, snatch-and-grab rough-ness but true tenderness with it or—

GEORGE: O.K., build yourself up! If that's what you need to!

RALPH: Naw, now, lissen! You know I know what I'm sayin'!

GEORGE: Sure, self-regarded expert!

[*They are both pretty high now.*]

RALPH: I know what went wrong last night at that Cape Girardeau motel as well as if I had seen it all on TV!

GEORGE: What went wrong is that I found myself hitched up with a woman in the "cut-it-off" category!

[ISABEL *is listening to all this in the bedroom. She stands up and sits down, stands up and sits down, barely able to keep from shouting something.*]

RALPH: Aw, naw, aw, naw. I will tell you what happened. Drink your champagne. What happened, man, is this! You didn't appreciate the natural need for using some tenderness with it. Lacking confidence with it, you wanted to hit her, smash her, clobber her with it. You've got violence in you! That's what made you such a good fighter pilot, the best there was! Sexual violence, that's what gives you the shakes, that's what makes you unstable. That's what made you just sit on the straw mats with the Tokyo dolls, drinking sake with them, teaching them English till it was time to come downstairs and holler, "Oh, man, oh, brother" like you had laid them to waste!

[*There is a slight pause.* GEORGE *is sweating, flushed.*]

GEORGE: Who in hell ever told you I—

RALPH: I heard it directly from them. You just sat up there drinkin' sake with 'em an' teachin' 'em English, and then you'd come down shouting, "Oh, man, oh, brother!" like you had laid 'em to waste.

GEORGE: Which of them told you this story?

RALPH: *Which* of them? ALL! EV'RY ONE!

[*They pause.* ISABEL *sits down on the bed again, raises her hands to either side of her face, slowly shaking her head with a gradual comprehension.*]

GEORGE: Man, at this moment I'd like to bust your face in!

RALPH: I'm tryin' to help you. Don't you know that I am tryin' t' help you?

[*A pause. They look away from each other in solemn reverie for some moments.* ISABEL *rises again from the bed but still doesn't move. After some moments she sits back down. She is crying now.*]

[RALPH, *continuing gently:*] You have got this problem.

GEORGE: In Tokyo I never told you—

RALPH: What?

GEORGE: I was choosy. I had a girl on the side. I mean a nice one. One that I wanted to keep to myself, strictly. I didn't want to expose her to a bunch of—

RALPH: Aw, now, man, you don't have to start fabricating some kind of a *Sayonara* fantasy like this!

GEORGE: How about Big Springs, Texas?

RALPH: What about Big Springs, Texas, besides being boring, I mean, what *else* about it?

GEORGE: Plenty. I fixed you up there. You never got nowhere in Big Springs, Texas, till I opened it up for you.

RALPH: Baby, don't be sore.

GEORGE: Sore, I'm not sore. You've done your damndest to make me feel like a phony, but I'm not sore. *You're* sore. Not *me. I'm* not sore.

RALPH: You sure are shaking.

GEORGE: Yeah, well, I got this tremor. . . . Jesus, my goddam voice is got the shakes too! But you know it's the truth, in Big Springs, Texas, we had the best damn time you ever had in your life, and I broke the ice there, for you.

86

RALPH: I don't deny that women naturally like you. Everybody likes you! Don't you know that? People never low-rate you! Don't you know that? I like you. That's for sure. But I hate to see you shaking because of—

GEORGE [*cutting in*]: Look! We're both free now. Like two birds. You're gonna cut out of this High Point over a Cavern. And we'll buy us a piece of ranchland near San Antone and both of us—

RALPH: Yeah, yeah, let's go back to what we wuh tawkin' about. *Tenderness.* With a *woman.*

GEORGE: I don't want to hear a goddam lecture from you about such a thing as that when here you are, night before Christmas, with just a cocker spaniel and presents under a tree, with no one to *take* them from you!

RALPH [*abruptly*]: *Hey!*

GEORGE: *Huh?*

RALPH: Th' *dawg* is back. How *come?*

GEORGE: The dawg come *back,* tha's all. . . .

[ISABEL *comes out of the bedroom in coat and hat.*]

ISABEL: Yes, I brought the dog back.

[*A pause, rather long.*]

RALPH: We, uh, we—saw you going up to the wrong— Spanish-type cottage. . . .

ISABEL: I haven't discovered the *right* one, Mr. Bates.

RALPH: I ain't discovered it either.

GEORGE: What kept you so long in the wrong one?

87

ISABEL: They invited me in and made me sit down to a lovely buffet supper while they looked up the High Point Bates in the phone book.

[*She pauses.*]

I heard your very enlightening conversation from the bedroom. You're a pair of small boys. Boasting, bragging, showing off to each other. . . . I want to call a cab. I'm going downtown, George.

[*He crosses unsteadily to the phone, lifts it and hands it to her with an effort at stateliness.*]

Thank you.

[*To* RALPH]

Do you know the cab number?

GEORGE: Whacha want, yellow, checkered or what? I'll git it for yuh!

RALPH: Put down th' phone.

ISABEL: I'll get one.

[*He dials the operator.*]

GEORGE: Leave her alone. Let her go downtown. She's free to.

[RALPH *takes the phone from her and puts it back in the cradle.*]

ISABEL: Do I have to walk?

[*She goes to the door, opens it and starts out.*]

There's a car in front of your house, Mr. Bates.

RALPH [*rising with sudden energy and rushing to the door*]: YEP! IT'S HER OLD MAN'S CAR! Dorothea's papa, my ex-boss!

ISABEL: Perhaps he'll be kind enough to—

RALPH: Go back in, little lady! Stay in the bedroom till I git through this! Then I'll drive you downtown if you're still determined to go.

[*He has drawn her back in the house.*]

SET DOWN, GEORGE! For Chrissakes. Little lady, will you please wait in the bedroom till I get through this hassle with her old man?

ISABEL: It's all so ridiculous. Yes, all right, I will, but please don't forget your promise to take me downtown right afterwards, Mr. Bates!

[*She returns to the bedroom with dignity.* MR. *and* MRS. MCGILLICUDDY *appear before the house.*

[*They are a pair of old bulls.*]

MRS. MCGILLICUDDY: The first thing to discuss is their joint savings account.

[MR. MCGILLICUDDY *hammers the knocker on the door.*]

I wish you'd listened to me an' brought your lawyer.

MR. MCGILLICUDDY: I can handle that boy. You keep your mouth out of it. Just collect the silver and china and let me handle the talk.

[*He knocks again, violently, dislodging the Christmas wreath attached to the knocker.* MRS. MCGILLICUDDY *picks it up.*]

Now what are you gonna do with that Christmas wreath? You gonna crown him with it?

[RALPH *opens the door.*]

RALPH: Well, Mr. and Mrs. *Mac!*

MR. MCGILLICUDDY [*handing him the wreath*]: This come off your knocker.

RALPH: Ha, ha, what a surprise!

MRS. MCGILLICUDDY: We've come to pick up some things of Dorothea's.

RALPH: That's O.K. Take out anything that's hers, but don't touch nothing that belongs to us both.

MRS. MCGILLICUDDY: We've come with a list of things that belong exclusively to Dorothea!

MR. MCGILLICUDDY: Is it true that you called up Emory Sparks at the place you quit your job at and asked him to come over here tonight and make you a cash-on-the-barrel offer for everything in this house?

RALPH: Nope.

MR. MCGILLICUDDY: Then how come Emory's fiancée called up Dorothea to give her that information?

MRS. MCGILLICUDDY [*impatiently*]: Come on in here, Susie.

[SUSIE *is the colored maid. She enters with a large laundry basket.*]

Is that the biggest basket you could find?

SUSIE: Yes, ma'am, it's the laundry basket.

MRS. MCGILLICUDDY: It isn't the large one. You'll have to make several trips up and down those slippery front steps with that little basket.

MR. MCGILLICUDDY: Haven't you got any ice-cream salt?

RALPH: You want to make some ice cream?

MR. MCGILLICUDDY: Susie, before you go down those steps with my daughter's china, you'd better collect some clinkers out of the furnace in the basement.

RALPH: How is she going to get clinkers out of an oil-burning furnace?

MR. MCGILLICUDDY: Oh, that's right. You burn oil. I forgot about that. Well, Susie, you better tote the basket of china down the terrace. Don't try to make the steps with it.

RALPH: She's not takin' no china out of this house.

MR. MCGILLICUDDY: You're not going to sell a goddam thing of my daughter's in this house!

RALPH: All I done was call up Emory Sparks because he's about to get married and invited him over to take a look at this place because I've got to unload it and I can't wait a couple of months to—

MR. MCGILLICUDDY: Now, hold on a minute, war hero!

RALPH: I don't like the way you always call me war hero!

MR. MCGILLICUDDY: *Why?* Ain't that what you *were?*

GEORGE: You're goddam right he was! I flown over seventy bombing missions with this boy in Korea and before that in the—

MR. MCGILLICUDDY: Yes, yes, yes, I know it backwards and forwards, and I know who you are. You are Haverstick, ain't you?

91

172212

GEORGE: Yeah, you got my name right.

MR. MCGILLICUDDY: Well, Haverstick, the war's over and you two bombers are grounded. Now, Susie, go in the kitchen and get that Mixmaster and that new Rotisserie out in the basket while I collect the silver in that sideboard in there.

RALPH: Susie, don't go in my kitchen. You want to be arrested for trespassing, Susie?

MRS. MCGILLICUDDY: Stuart, you'd better call that policeman in here.

RALPH: NO KIDDING!

MRS. MCGILLICUDDY: We anticipated that you'd make trouble.

RALPH: How does Dorothea feel about you all doing this?

MR. MCGILLICUDDY [*at the door*]: OFFICER!—He's coming.

RALPH: How does Dotty feel? What is her attitude toward this kind of—

[*He is trembling. His voice chokes.* GEORGE *rises and puts a hand on Ralph's shoulder as a young* POLICE OFFICER *enters looking embarrassed.*]

MR. MCGILLICUDDY: You know the situation, Lieutenant. We have to remove my daughter's valuables from the house because we've been tipped off this man here, Ralph Bates, is intending to make a quick cash sale of everything in the house and skip out of Dixon tomorrow.

RALPH: THAT'S A GODDAM LIE! WHO TOLD YOU THAT?

MRS. MCGILLICUDDY: Emory Sparks' fiancée is Dorothea's good friend! That's how we got the warning. She called to enquire if Dorothea was serious about this matter. How did

92

Dotty feel, how did she FEEL? I'll tell you! SICK AT HER
STOMACH! VIOLENTLY SICK AT HER STOMACH.

RALPH: I should think so, goddam it. I should THINK so!
She's got many a fault she got from you two, but, hell, she'd
never agree to a piece of cheapness like this any more'n she'd
believe that story about me callin'—

MR. MCGILLICUDDY: How could there be any possible
doubt about it when Emory Sparks' fiancée—

RALPH: Will you allow me to speak? I did call Emory
Sparks and told him my wife had quit me because I had quit
my job, and I merely suggested that he come over and kind
of look over the stuff here and see if any of all this goddam
electric equipment and so forth would be of any use to him
since it isn't to me and since I got to have some financial—

[*He becomes suddenly speechless and breathless.* GEORGE
embraces his shoulder.]

GEORGE: Now, now, son, this is going to work out. Don't
blow a gasket over it.

RALPH: I think you folks had better consider some legal
angles of what you're up to here.

MR. MCGILLICUDDY [*puffing, red in the face*]: Aw, there's
no legal angle about it that I don't know, and if there was, I
could cope with that, too. I'm prepared to cope with that
trouble. You got no goddam position in this town but what
I give you!

RALPH: *Oh!* Uh-huh—

[MRS. MCGILLICUDDY *has gone to the bedroom and discovered* ISABEL *in it.*]

MRS. MCGILLICUDDY: *Stuart, they have a woman in Dotty's
bedroom!*

93

RALPH: George's wife is in there.

MRS. MCGILLICUDDY: How long have you been planning this?

[*She knocks on the bedroom door.*]

Can I come in?

ISABEL: Yes, please.

[MRS. MCGILLICUDDY *enters the bedroom.*]

MRS. MCGILLICUDDY [*coldly*]: I've come to pick up some things that belong to my daughter.

ISABEL: I told my husband we'd dropped in at the wrong time.

MRS. MCGILLICUDDY: May I ask who you are?

ISABEL: I'm Mrs. George Haverstick. You probably saw my husband in the front room.

MRS. MCGILLICUDDY: Your husband's an old friend of Ralph's, one of his wartime buddies?

ISABEL: Yes, he is, Mrs.— I didn't get your name.

MRS. MCGILLICUDDY: All I can say is "Watch out," if he's an old friend of Ralph's!

ISABEL: Why?

MRS. MCGILLICUDDY: Birds of a feather, that's all.

[MRS. MCGILLICUDDY *opens the closet and starts piling clothes on the bed. In the living room,* MR. MCGILLICUDDY *takes a seat in silence.*]

ISABEL: Are you sure you're doing the right thing?

MRS. MCGILLICUDDY [*calling out the door*] Susie!

94

SUSIE [*entering*]: Yes, ma'am?

MRS. MCGILLICUDDY: Take these clothes of Miss Dotty's out to the car.

[SUSIE *carries out the clothes.*]

ISABEL: I think young people should be given a chance to work things out by themselves.

MRS. MCGILLICUDDY: You have no idea at all of the situation. And I'm sure you have your own problems if you have married a friend of my daughter's husband. Is he living on his war record like Ralph Bates is?

ISABEL: He has a distinguished war record and a nervous disability that was a result of seventy-two flying missions in Korea and, and—more than twice that many in—

MRS. MCGILLICUDDY: *I'm sick of hearing about past glories! Susie!*

[SUSIE *comes in again.*]

Now pick up all Dotty's shoes on the floor of that closet, put 'em in the bottom of the basket, put some paper over them, and then pile her little undies on top of the paper.— Then! If you still have room in the basket, collect some of the china out of the sideboard and cupboards. Be very careful with that. Don't try to carry too much at one time, Susie. That walk and those steps are a hazard.

[*There has been a prolonged silence in the front room during the scene above, which they have been listening to.*]

MR. MCGILLICUDY [*at last*]: Well, you seem to be living the life of Riley. French champagne. Who was the little girl I saw come out and go back in?

RALPH: Mrs. George Haverstick.

MR. MCGILLICUDDY: That means as much to me as if you said she was a lady from Mars.

RALPH: There's no reason why it should mean anything to you. I just answered your question.

MR. MCGILLICUDDY: Why do you feel so superior to me?

RALPH: Aw. Did you notice that?

MR. MCGILLICUDDY: From the first time I met you. You have always acted very superior to me for some unknown reason. I'd like to know what it is. You were employed by me till you quit your job today.

RALPH: Does that mean I had to feel inferior to you, Mac?

MR. MCGILLICUDDY: You've started calling me "Mac"?

RALPH: I'm not employed by you, now.

MR. MCGILLICUDDY: If there was a war you could be a war hero again, but in a cold war I don't see how you're going to be such a hero. A cold-war hero, ha ha, is not such a hero, at least not in the newspapers.

[*Gathering confidence*]

Huh? Why don't you answer my question?

RALPH: Which, Mac?

MR. MCGILLICUDDY: Why you feel so rutten superior to me.

RALPH: Can I consider that question? For a minute?

MR. MCGILLICUDDY: Yeah, consider it, will you? I fail to see anything *special* about you, war hero!

[*He lights a cigar with jerky motions. The two younger men stare at his red, puffy face with intolerant smiles*]

96

GEORGE: Let me answer for him. He feels superior to you because you're a big male cow, a spiritual male cow.

RALPH: Shut up, George. Well, Mr. Mac? Let me ask you a question. Why did you ask me to marry your daughter?

MR. MCGILLICUDDY: DID WHAT? I NEVER! Done any such thing and—

[MRS. MCGILLICUDDY *snorts indignantly from the open bedroom door.*]

RALPH: You mean to say you've forgotten that you suggested to me that I marry Dotty?

[MRS. MCGILLICUDDY *advances from the bedroom door, bearing a French porcelain clock.*]

MR. MCGILLICUDDY: I never forgotten a thing in my adult life, but I never have any such recollections as that. I do remember a conversation I held with you soon after you started to work at Regal Dairy Products an' come to my office to quit because you said you weren't gittin' paid well enough an' th' work was monotonous to you.

RALPH: That's right. Five years ago this winter.

MR. MCGILLICUDDY: I gave you a fatherly talk. I told you monotony was a part of life. And I said I had an eye on you, which I did at that time.

RALPH: How about the rest of the conversation? In which you said that Dotty was your only child, that you had no son, and Dotty was int'rested in me and if Dotty got married her husband would be the heir to your throne as owner of Regal Dairy an' its subsidiaries such as Royal Ice Cream and Monarch Cheese, huh?

MRS. MCGILLICUDDY: HANH!

97

RALPH: An' you hadn't long for this world because of acute diabetes and so forth and—

MRS. MCGILLICUDDY: HANH!

RALPH: And I would be shot right into your shoes when you departed this world? Well, you sure in hell lingered!

MRS. MCGILLICUDDY: ARE YOU GOING TO STAND THERE LISTENING TO THIS, STUART? I'M NOT!

MR. MCGILLICUDDY: Be still, Mama. I can talk for myself. I did discuss these things with you but how did you arrive at the idea I asked you to marry my daughter?

MRS. MCGILLICUDDY: HANH!

[GEORGE *goes to look out the window as if the scene had ceased to amuse him.*]

RALPH: What other way could it be interpreted, Mac?

[*He is no longer angry.*]

MR. MCGILLICUDDY: I offered you a splendid chance in the world which you spit on by your disrespect, your superior—!

RALPH: I respect Dorothea. Always did and still do.

MR. MCGILLICUDDY: I'm talkin' about your attitude to me.

RALPH: I know you are. That's all that you care about, not about Dorothea. You don't love Dotty. She let you down by having psychological problems that you brought on her, that you an' Mrs. Mac gave her by pushing her socially past her social endowments.

MRS. MCGILLICUDDY: WHAT DO YOU MEAN BY THAT?

RALPH: Dotty was never cut out to boost your social position in this city. Which you expected her to. You made her feel inferior all her life.

MRS. MCGILLICUDDY: *Me? Me?*

RALPH: Both of yuh. I respected her, though, and sincerely liked her and I married Dotty. Give me credit for that, and provided her with an—offspring. Maybe not much of an offspring, but an offspring, a male one, at least it started a male one. I can't help it if she's turnin' him into a sissy, I—

MRS. MCGILLICUDDY: MY GOD, STUART, HOW LONG ARE YOU GONNA STAND THERE AND LISTEN TO THIS WITHOUT—

MR. MCGILLICUDDY: *Mama, I told you to keep your mouth outa this!*

RALPH: Yeah, but I MARRIED your baby. Give me credit for that. And provided her with an—offspring!

MRS. MCGILLICUDDY: What does he mean by that? That *he* had the baby, not Dotty?

MR. MCGILLICUDDY: Mama, I told you to keep your mouth out of this.

MRS. MCGILLICUDDY: He talks like he thought he did Dotty a FAVOR!

RALPH: Now, listen. I don't want to be forced into saying unkind things about Dotty. But you all know damn well that Dotty was half a year older than me when I married that girl and if I hadn't you would have been stuck with a lonely, unmarried daughter for the rest of your lives!

MRS. MCGILLICUDDY: *Oh,* my—GOD!

MR. MCGILLICUDDY: Let him talk. I want to hear all, all, all! he has to say about Dotty.

RALPH: You're *going* to hear it, if you stay in my house! I put up a five-year battle between our marriage and your goddam hold on her! You just wouldn't release her!—although I doubt that you wanted her always unmarried.

99

MRS. MCGILLICUDDY: WHAT MAKES YOU THINK SHE WOULD HAVE STAYED UNMARRIED?

RALPH: The indications, past history, when I met her—

MRS. MCGILLICUDDY: This is too sickening. I can't stand it, Stuart?

MR. MCGILLICUDDY: A bum like you?

RALPH: Don't call *me* a bum!

MR. MCGILLICUDDY: What in hell else *are* you? I give you your job which you quit today without warning! Carried you in it despite your indifference to it for—for—for—five—

RALPH: Wait! Like I said. I still respect your daughter, don't want to say anything not kind about her, but let's face facts. Who else but a sucker like me, Ralph Bates, would have married a girl with no looks, a plain, homely girl that probably no one but me had ever felt anything but just— SORRY FOR!

MRS. MCGILLICUDDY: OH GOD! STUART, ARE YOU GOING TO STAND THERE AND LET HIM GO ON WITH THAT TALK?

RALPH: HOW IN HELL DO YOU FIGURE HE'S GOING TO STOP ME?

MRS. MCGILLICUDDY: OFFICER! CAN'T YOU GET THIS MAN OUT OF HERE?

OFFICER: No, ma'am. I can't arrest him.

RALPH: ARREST ME FOR WHAT, MRS. MAC?

GEORGE: That's right, arrest him for what?

MRS. MCGILLICUDDY: Stuart? Take out the silver. I don't know where Susie is. We should have come here with your lawyer as well as this—*remarkably—incompetent—policeman!*

MR. MCGILLICUDDY: Susie took out the silver.

GEORGE: Naw, she didn't. I got the goddam silver. I'm sitting on it!

[*He sits on silver, then rises and stuffs it under sofa pillow, having been discomfited by the forks.*]

MR. MCGILLICUDDY: I guess I'll have to call the Chief of Police, who's a lodge brother of mine, and get a little more police co-operation than we have gotten so far.

OFFICER: O.K., you do that, Mister.

MR. MCGILLICUDDY: He'll call you to the phone and give you exact instructions.

OFFICER: That's all right. If he gives 'em, I'll take 'em.

[MRS. MCGILLICUDDY *has charged back into the bedroom to collect more things.*]

RALPH: Mr. McGillicuddy, you are the worst thing any person can be: mean-minded, small-hearted, and CHEAP! Outstandingly and notoriously cheap! It was almost two months before I could *kiss* Dorothea, sincerely, after meeting her father! That's no crap. It wasn't the homeliness that threw me, it was the association she had in my mind with *you!* It wasn't till I found out she despised you as much as I did that I was able to make real love to Dotty.

MR. MCGILLICUDDY: My daughter is *crazy* about me!

RALPH: You're crazy if you *think* so!

[MRS. MCGILLICUDDY *comes out of the bedroom.*]

MRS. MCGILLICUDDY: All right. All of Dotty's clothes have been taken out. I think we may as well leave now.

101

MR. MCGILLICUDDY: How about the TV? Which I gave Dotty *last* Christmas?

RALPH: You want the TV? O.K.! Here's the TV!

[*He shoves it to the door and pulls the door open.*]

Take the TV out of here—an' git out with it!

MRS. MCGILLICUDDY: What is that under the tree? It looks like a new fur coat!

RALPH: That's right. A seven-hundred-and-forty-five-dollar sheared-beaver coat that I'd bought for Dotty for Christmas! —but which I have just now presented to Mrs. George Haverstick as her weddin' present.

MR. MCGILLICUDDY: The hell you have! How did you git hold of seven hundred and—

RALPH: From my savings account.

MR. MCGILLICUDDY: That was a *joint* account!

MRS. MCGILLICUDDY: STUART! TAKE THAT COAT! GO ON, PICK UP THAT COAT!

RALPH: By God, if he touches that coat, I'll smash him into next week, and I never hit an old man before in my life.

MRS. MCGILLICUDDY: OFFICER! PICK UP THAT COAT!

RALPH: I'll hit any man that tries to pick up that coat!

OFFICER [*putting down the phone, which he has been talking into quietly*]:

I talked to my chief. He gave me my instructions. He says not to take any action that might result in publicity, because of Mr. Bates having been a very well-known war hero.

MR. MCGILLICUDDY: Come on, Mama. I'll just have to re-
fer this whole disgusting business to my lawyer tomorrow,
put it all in his hands and get the necessary papers to protect
our baby.

MRS. MCGILLICUDDY: I just want to say one thing more!
Ralph Bates, don't you think for a moment that you are going
to escape financial responsibility for the support of your child!
Now come on, Stuart!—Isn't it pitiful? All that little boy's
Christmas under the tree?

RALPH: Send him over tomorrow to pick it all up. That can
go out of the house, the little boy's Christmas can go. . . .

[*They all leave.* ISABEL *enters from bedroom.*]

ISABEL: Mr. Bates! I don't believe that this is what your
wife wanted. I'll also bet you that she is outside in that car
and if you would just stick your head out the window and
call her, she would come running in here.

[DOROTHEA *comes onto the paved terrace and knocks at
the door.* RALPH *does not move. She knocks again, harder
and longer. He starts to rise, sits down again.*]

George, let his wife in the house.

GEORGE: Let's just keep out of this. I reckon he knows
what he's doing.

[*A car honks. A* WOMAN'S VOICE *is heard.*]

WOMAN [*off*]: Dorothea! Come back! We'll get the police!

DOROTHEA [*calling at the door*]: Ralph? Ralph? It's
Dotty! I want the child's Christmas things!

RALPH: HE'LL GET THEM HERE OR NOWHERE!

DOROTHEA: *I'm not going to leave here without the child's
Christmas things!*—Ralph.

103

RALPH: *Let him come here alone tomorrow morning.*

DOROTHEA: *You can't do that to a child.*—Ralph!

[*The car honks again, long and loud.*]

RALPH [*shouting back*]: Put the kid in a taxi in the morning and I'll let him in to collect his Christmas presents!

MRS. MCGILLICUDDY [*appearing behind Dorothea*]: Dorothea! I will not let you humiliate yourself like this! Come away from that door!

DOROTHEA: Mama, stay in the car!

WOMAN: Your father won't wait any longer. He's started the car. He's determined to get the police.

DOROTHEA: RALPH! [*She has removed the door key from her bag.*] I'M COMING IN!

WOMAN: *Dotty, where is your pride!*

[DOROTHEA *enters and slams the door. The* WOMAN *rushes off, crying "Stuart!"*]

[DOROTHEA *stares at Ralph from the door. He gazes stubbornly at the opposite wall.*]

DOROTHEA: I could tell you'd been drinkin' by your voice. Who are these people you've got staying in the house.

RALPH: Talk about the police! I could get you all arrested for illegal entry!

DOROTHEA: This is your liquor speaking, not you, Ralph.

RALPH: You have abandoned me. You got no right by law to come back into this house and make insulting remarks about my friends.

DOROTHEA: Ralph? Ralph? I know I acted—impetuously this mawnin'. . . .

RALPH: Naw, I think you made the correct decision. You realized that you had tied yourself down to a square peg in a round hole that had now popped out of the hole and consequently would be of no further use to you. You were perfectly satisfied for me to remain at that rutten little desk job, tyrannized over by inferior men, for as long as my—heart kept beating.

DOROTHEA: No, Ralph. I wasn't. MY aim for you was your aim. Independence! A business of your own!

RALPH: Not when you were *faced* with it.

DOROTHEA: You sprung it on me at the wrong moment, Ralph. Our savings account is at a very low ebb.

RALPH: Our savings account is all gone, little woman. It went on Christmas, all of it.

[*He pokes at the fire. There is a pause. The fire crackles and flickers.*]

DOROTHEA: *Mama* says you—bought me a *fur coat* for Christmas.

RALPH: Yeah, she took a look at it. Enquired the price. Wanted to take it off with her.

DOROTHEA: You wouldn't have bought me such a beautiful coat if you didn't still care for me, Ralph. You know that, don't you?

RALPH: I made a decision affecting my whole future life. I know it was a big step, but I had the courage to make it.

DOROTHEA: I've always admired your courage.

105

RALPH: Hah!—I break the news. You walked right out on me, Dotty, takin' my son that you've turned into a sissy. He won't want these boys' toys under that tree. What he'll want is a doll and a—*tea* set.

DOROTHEA: All of these things are a little too old for Ralph Junior but he'll be delighted with them just the same, Ralph.

[*She takes off her cloth coat.*]

I'm going to try on that wonderful-looking beaver.

RALPH: It's not going out of the house, off you or on you, Dotty.

[*She puts on the beaver-skin coat.*]

DOROTHEA: Oh, how lovely, how lovely! Ralph, it *does* prove you love me!

RALPH: It cleaned out our savings account.

DOROTHEA: Both of us have been guilty of impetuous actions. You must've been awfully lonely, inviting a pair of strangers to occupy our bedroom on Christmas Eve.

RALPH: George Haverstick is not any stranger to me. We both of us died in two wars, repeatedly died in two wars and were buried in suburbs named High Point, but his was hyphenated. H-i-hyphen-Point. Mine was spelled out but was built on a cavern for the daughter and grandchild of Mr. and Mrs. Stuart McGillicuddy. Oh, I told him something which I should have told you five years ago, Dorothea. I married you without love. I married you for—

DOROTHEA: Ralph? Please don't!

RALPH: I married you for your stingy-fisted old papa's promise to—

DOROTHEA: *Ralphie*! *Don't*! *I know*!

RALPH: —to make me his Heir Apparent! Assurances, lies! Even broad hints that he would soon kick off!

DOROTHEA: Ralph?

[*She puts her hand over his mouth, beseechingly.*]

Don't you know I know that?

RALPH: Why' you accept it? If you—

DOROTHEA: I was so—

[*She covers her face.*]

RALPH: Cut it out, have some pride!

DOROTHEA: I *do*!

RALPH: In *what*?

DOROTHEA: In *you*!

RALPH: Oh, for the love of— In me? Why, I'm telling you I'm nothin' better'n a goddam—

DOROTHEA: I know, don't tell me again. I always knew it. —I had my nose done over and my front teeth extracted to look better for you, Ralphie!

RALPH: "Ralphie!" *Shoot* . . .

[ISABEL *raps discreetly at the bedroom door.*]

Huh? What is it?

ISABEL: I've made some coffee.

DOROTHEA: I *did* improve my appearance, didn't I, Ralph? It was extremely painful.

107

RALPH: Don't claim you done it for me! Every woman wants to improve on nature any way that she can. Yes! Of course you look better! You think you've won a *argument?*

DOROTHEA: *Me? What* argument? *No!* I've come back *crawling!*—not even embarrassed to do so!

[ISABEL *comes in from the kitchenette with coffee.*]

Oh! Hello. I didn't know you were—

ISABEL: Mrs. Bates. I'm Isabel Haverstick. I took the liberty of making some coffee in your sweet little kitchen. Mrs. Bates, can I give you some coffee?

DOROTHEA: Thanks, that's awfully sweet of you, Mrs. Haverstick. It's nice of you and your husband to drop in on Ralph, but the situation between Ralph and me has changed. I guess I don't have to explain it. You see I've come home. We only have one bedroom and Ralph and I have an awful lot to talk over.

ISABEL: I understand perfectly. George and I are going to go right downtown.

DOROTHEA [*softening*]: You don't have to do that. This sofa lets out to a bed and it's actually more comfortable than the beds in the bedroom. I know, because other times when we've had a falling out, less serious than this time, I have—occupied it.

[*With a little, soft, sad, embarrassed laugh.*]

Of course, I usually called Ralph in before mawnin'. . . .

ISABEL: Oh, but this is no time for strangers to be here with you!

DOROTHEA [*now really warming*]: You all stay here! I insist! It's really not easy to get a hotel room downtown with so many folks coming into town for Christmas.

ISABEL: Well, if you're sure, if you're absolutely certain our presence wouldn't be inconvenient at all?—I do love this room. The fire is still burning bright!—and the Christmas tree is so—pretty.

DOROTHEA: I'll tell my mother and father, they're still outside in the car, to drive home and then we'll all have coffee together!

[*She rushes out in her beaver coat.*]

ISABEL: I like her! She's really nice!

RALPH: She came back for the fur coat.

ISABEL: I think she came back for you.

RALPH: She walked out on me this morning because I had liberated myself from a slave's situation!—and she took the kid with her.

ISABEL: You're just going through a—period of adjustment.

RALPH: We've been married six years.

ISABEL: But all that time you've been under terrible strain, hating what you were doing, and maybe taking it out on your wife, Ralph Bates.

[DOROTHEA *returns.*]

DOROTHEA: All right. I sent them home, much against their objections. I just slammed the car door on them.

RALPH: They comin' back with the police?

DOROTHEA: No. You know they were bluffing.

ISABEL: I think you two should have your coffee alone in your own little bedroom. We'll all get acquainted tomorrow.

DOROTHEA: Ralph?

RALPH [*sadly*]: I don't know. We're living over a cavern. . . .

[*He follows* DOROTHEA *into the bedroom. It remains dimly lighted.*]

DOROTHEA: But Mama's took all my things! I forgot to ask them back from her. I'll just have to sleep jay-bird since she took even my nighties.

RALPH: Yes, she was fast and thorough, but didn't get out with that seven-hundred-buck beaver coat.

DOROTHEA: I like your friends. But the girl looks terribly nervous. Well-bred, however, and the boy is certainly very good-looking!

RALPH: Thanks.

[*The bedroom dims out as* DOROTHEA *enters the bathroom. A silence has fallen between the pair in the living room.*]

ISABEL: Coffee, George?

GEORGE: No, thanks.

ISABEL: Moods change quickly, don't they?

GEORGE: Basic attitudes don't.

ISABEL: Yes, but it takes a long time to form basic attitudes and to know what they are, and meantime you just have to act according to moods.

GEORGE: Is that what you are acting according to, now?

ISABEL: I'm not acting according to anything at all now, I—

[*She sits on a hassock before the fireplace.*]

I don't think she came back just for the coat. Do you?

110

GEORGE: It's not my business. I don't have any opinion. If that was her reason, Ralph Bates will soon find it out.

ISABEL: Yes . . .

DOROTHEA [*at the door*]: Excuse me, may I come in?

ISABEL: Oh, please.

DOROTHEA [*entering*]: Mama took all my *things*! Have you got an extra nightie that I could borrow?

ISABEL: Of course I have.

DOROTHEA: I forgot to take anything back. . . .

[ISABEL *opens her overnight bag and extends a gossamer nightgown to Dorothea.*]

Oh! How exquisite! No!—that's your honeymoon nightie. Just give me any old plain one!

ISABEL: Really, I have two of them, exactly alike. Please take it!

DOROTHEA: Are you sure?

ISABEL: I'm positive. You take it!

[*She holds up another.*]

See? The same thing exactly, just a different color. I gave you the blue one and kept the pink one for me.

DOROTHEA: Oh. Well, thank you so much.

ISABEL: If you'd prefer the pink one—?

DOROTHEA: I'm delighted with the blue one! Well, g'night, you folks. Sweet dreams.

[*She returns to the dark bedroom.* RALPH *is prone and motionless on the bed. A tiny light spills from the bath-*

room door. DOROTHEA *enters the bathroom and closes the door so the bedroom turns pitch-black.*]

GEORGE [*grimly*]: D'ya want me to go outside while you undress?

ISABEL: No, I, I—I'm—just going ot take off my *suit*. I—I, I have a *slip* on, I—

[*She gives him a quick, scared look. The removal of her suit is almost panickily self-conscious and awkward.*]

GEORGE: Well. Ralph and I have decided to—

ISABEL [*fearfully*]: *What?*

GEORGE [*finishes his drink, then goes on*]: Ralph and I have decided to go in the cattle business, near San Antone.

ISABEL: Who is going to finance it?

[*She has turned out the lamp.*]

GEORGE: We think we can work it out. We have to be smart, and lucky. Just smart and lucky.

[ISABEL *drops her skirt to her feet and stands before the flickering fireplace in a slip that the light makes transparent.*]

ISABEL: We all have to be smart and lucky. Or unlucky and silly.

[DOROTHEA *comes out of the bathroom. Light from the bathroom brightens the bedroom, where* RALPH *is slowly undressing.*]

RALPH: All right, you're back. But a lot has been discussed and decided on since you cut out of here, Dotty.

DOROTHEA [*picks up something on the dresser*]: Good! What?

RALPH: Please don't rub that Vick's Vap-O-Rub on your chest.

DOROTHEA: I'm *not*! This is Hind's honey-almond cream for my *hands*!

RALPH: Aw.

[*She starts taking off her shoes.*

[*In the living room:*]

GEORGE: What're you up to?

ISABEL: Up to?

GEORGE: Standin' in front of that fire with that transparent thing on you. You must know it's transparent.

ISABEL: I honestly didn't even think about that.

[ISABEL *crouches by the fire, holding her delicate hands out to its faint, flickering glow.*

[*In the bedroom:*]

RALPH: All right. Here it is. George and me are going to cash in every bit of collateral we possess, including the beaver-skin coat and his fifty-two Caddy to buy a piece of ranchland near San Antone.

DOROTHEA: Oh. What are you planning to do on this—

RALPH: —ranch? Breed cattle. Texas Longhorns.
[*A pause.*]

DOROTHEA: I like animals, Ralph.

RALPH: Cocker spaniels.

DOROTHEA: No, I like horses, too. I took equitation at Sophie Newcomb's. I even learned how to post.

113

RALPH: Uh-huh.

DOROTHEA: For a little ole Texas girl she sure does have some mighty French taste in nighties!

RALPH: I don't imagine she suffers from psychological frigidity.

DOROTHEA: Honey, I never suffered from that. Did you believe I really suffered from that?

RALPH: When your father proposed to me—

DOROTHEA: Ralph, don't say things like that! Don't, don't humiliate me!

RALPH: Honey, I—

DOROTHEA: PLEASE don't humiliate me by—

RALPH: HONEY!

[*He goes up to her at the dressing table. Sobbing, she presses her head against him.*]

You KNOW I respect you, honey.

ISABEL [*in the other room*]: What an awful, frightening thing it is!

GEORGE: What?

ISABEL: Two people living together, two, two—different worlds!—attempting—existence—together!

[*In the bedroom:*]

RALPH: Honey, will you stop?

DOROTHEA: Respect me, respect me, is that all you can give me when I've loved you so much that sometimes I shake all over at the sight or touch of you? Still? Now? Always?

114

RALPH: The human heart would never pass the drunk test.

DOROTHEA: Huh?

RALPH: If you took the human heart out of the human body and put a pair of legs on it and told it to walk a straight line, it couldn't do it. It never could pass the drunk test.

DOROTHEA: I love you, baby. And I love animals, too. Hawses, spaniels, longhorns!

RALPH: The Texas longhorn is a—dignified beast.

DOROTHEA: You say that like you thought it was TOO GOOD FOR ME!

RALPH: How do I know that you didn't just come back here for that sheared beaver coat?

[*Living room:*]

ISABEL: I hope they're getting things ironed out between them.

GEORGE: Why?

ISABEL: They need each other. That's why.

GEORGE: Let's mind our own business, huh?

[*Bedroom:*]

DOROTHEA: You'll just have to WONDER! And WONDER!

[*Living room:*]

GEORGE: It's a parallel situation. They're going through a period of adjustment just like us.

[*Bedroom:*]

RALPH: All my life, huh?

115

DOROTHEA: And I'll have to wonder, too, if you love me, Ralph. There's an awful lot of wondering between people.

RALPH: Come on. Turn out the light. Let's go to bed-ville, baby.

DOROTHEA [*turning out the light*]: His or hers?

RALPH: In West Texas we'll get a big one called OURS!

[*In the living room,* GEORGE *has turned on TV and a chorus is singing "White Christmas."*]

GEORGE: Aw. You hate "White Christmas."

[*He turns it down.*]

ISABEL: I don't hate it now, baby.

[*He turns it back up, but softly.*]

DOROTHEA: I'm lookin' *forward* to it. I always wanted a big one, OURS!

RALPH: There's more dignity in it.

DOROTHEA: *Yes!*

[*She giggles breathlessly in the dark.*]

ISABEL [*in the living room*]: I think they've talked things over and are working things out.

[*Bedroom:*]

RALPH: Yes. It makes it easy to know if—I mean, you don't have to wonder if—

[DOROTHEA *giggles in the dark.*]

That long, long, dangerous walk between "His" and "Hers" can be accomplished, or not. . . .

[*Living room:*]

116

ISABEL: I didn't know until now that the shakes are catching! Why do you keep standing up and sitting back down like a big old jack-in-the-box?

[*A low rumble is heard. It builds. Something falls off a shelf in the kitchenette. Crockery rattles together.*]

WHAT'S THIS!?

GEORGE: Aw, nothin', nothin'.

RALPH [*entering the doorway*]: Well, she jus' slipped again!

DOROTHEA [*appearing behind him*]: Did you all feel that tremor?

ISABEL: Yes, it felt like an earthquake.

DOROTHEA: We get those little tremors all the time because it seems that this suburb is built over a huge underground cavern and is sinking into it, bit by bit. That's the secret of how we could afford to buy this nice little home of ours at such a knockdown price.

ISABEL: It isn't likely to fall in the cavern *tonight?*

DOROTHEA: No. They say it's going to be gradual, about half an inch every year. Do you all mind if I turn on the light a second to see if there's any new cracks?

ISABEL: No, I'll—put on my robe.

[*She does. The room is lighted.*]

DOROTHEA: Yais! Ralph? A *new* one! This one is a jim-dandy, all the way 'cross the ceiling! See it, honey? All the way 'cross the ceiling. Well—

[*A pause.*]

117

We will leave you alone now. I still feel badly about you having to sleep on that folding contraption.

RALPH: Anything I can do? Anything I can—

DOROTHEA: Ralph! Leave them alone. Merry Christmas!

[*She shuts the door.*]

[*Pause.* ISABEL *stands before fireplace in the fourth wall.*

[*Pause.*]

GEORGE: Isabel? Little Bit? Marriage is a big step for a man to take, especially when he's—nervous. I'm pretty—nervous.

ISABEL: I know.

GEORGE: For a man with the shakes, especially, it's a—big step to take, it's—

ISABEL: I know what you're trying to tell me.

GEORGE [*taking seat on high stool near fire*]: Do you, honey?

[*He looks up at her quickly, then down.*]

ISABEL: Of course I do. I expect all men are a little bit nervous about the same thing.

GEORGE: What?

ISABEL: About how they'll be at love-making.

GEORGE: Yeah, well, they don't have the shakes. I mean, not all the others have got a nervous tremor like I've got.

ISABEL: Inside or outside, they've all got a nervous tremor of some kind, sweetheart. The world is a big hospital, and I am a nurse in it, George. The whole world's a big hospital, a big neurological ward and I am a student nurse in it. I

118

guess that's still my job!—I love this fire. It feels so good on my skin through this little pink slip. I'm glad she left me the *pink* nightie, tonight.

GEORGE [*huskily*]: Yeah, I'm glad she did, too.

[ISABEL *retires to slip into her nightgown.*]

I wish I had that—little electric buzzer I—had at—Barnes. . . .

ISABEL: You don't need a buzzer. I'm not way down at the end of a corridor, baby. If you call me, I'll hear you.

[*She returns and hugs her knees, sitting before the fireplace. He rests his head on his cupped hands. She begins to sing softly:*]

> "Now the boat goes round the bend,
> Good-by, my lover, good-by,
> It's loaded down with boys and men,
> Good-by, my lover, good-by!"

RALPH [*in the dark other room*]: She's singin'!

[*Pause.*]

DOROTHEA: Papa said you told him that I was—homely! Did you say that, Ralph? That I was homely?

RALPH: Dotty, you used to be homely but you improved in appearance.

DOROTHEA: You never told me you thought I was homely, Ralph.

RALPH: I just meant you had a off-beat kind of face, honey, but—the rest of you is attractive.

DOROTHEA [*giggles*]: I always knew *I* was homely but you were good enough lookin' to make *up* for it! Baby—

119

[ISABEL *is singing again, a little forlornly, by the fireplace.*]

ISABEL:
"Bye low, my baby!   Bye low, my baby!
Bye low, my baby! Good-by, my lover, good-by!"

[GEORGE *whistles softly.*]

Was that for me?

GEORGE: Come here!

ISABEL: No, you come here. It's very nice by the fire.

[*In the other room, as the curtain begins to fall:*]

DOROTHEA: Careful, let me do it!—It isn't mine!

[*She means the borrowed nightgown.*]

[*In the front room,* GEORGE *has risen from the bed and is crossing to the fireplace as:*]

THE CURTAIN FALLS

Date Due